2021

QUANTUM HUMAN DESIGN EVOLUTION GUIDE

Using Solar Transits to Design Your Year

KAREN CURRY PARKER

2021
QUANTUM HUMAN DESIGN
EVOLUTION GUIDE

Using Solar Transits to Design Your Year

KAREN CURRY PARKER

Please visit QuantumAlignmentSystem.com for more information about Quantum Human Design, to see a list of our Certified Specialists, and for additional valuable resources.

@HumanDesignForEveryone

@understandinghumandesign

www.quantumalignmentsystem.com

An Imprint for GracePoint Publishing (www.GracePointPublishing.com)
GracePoint Matrix, LLC
322 N Tejon St. #207
Colorado Springs CO 80903
www.GracePointMatrix.com
Email: Admin@GracePointMatrix.com
SAN # 991-6032

ISBN-13: (Paperback) #978-1-951694-32-6

eISBN: (eBook) #978-1-951694-31-9

Books may be purchased for educational, business, or sales promotional use.
For bulk order requests and price schedule contact:
Orders@GracePointPublishing.com
Printed in the United States of America

For more great books on Human Design, please visit our online store!

HUMAN
DESIGN
PRESS

DEDICATION

To all my students, Quantum Human Design Specialists, and Quantum Alignment Practitioners. Thank you for trusting me to be your teacher. Thank you for sharing the gift of Who You Truly Are with the world. I am because you are. I love you!

CONTENTS

INTRODUCTION

This book is a weekly guide designed to give you a deliberate way to harness the energy of the Sun and the Moon to support you in creating what you want in your life.

Quantum Human Design is a collection of cross-cultural, ancient and modern archetypes. An archetype is a pattern of thought or symbolic image that is derived from the past collective experience of humanity.

We experience all of the archetypes in the human design charts, either from our own unique charts, our relationships or through the planetary transits.

The colored in or "defined" elements in your Human Design chart tell you which archetypes you carry in your own chart. The "defined" elements in your chart are part of what you must master to bring your gifts into the world.

The white or "undefined" elements in your Human Design chart tell you a lot about what you are here to learn from others and from the world. You will experience these archetypes in a variety of different ways depending on who you are with and what energies are transiting in the celestial weather.

Over the course of a calendar year, the Sun moves through all 64 of the Human Design Gates. The Human Design Gates contain the energy code for 64 core human archetypes. As the sun moves through an archetype, it "lights up" that theme for everyone on the planet, creating a theme for the week.

We all deal with the weekly themes. Even if the theme doesn't impact your chart deeply, it will impact the charts of the people around you. The gift of the solar transits is that it gives you an opportunity to work deliberately with all 64 of these core human archetypes and to consciously focus on living the highest expression of these energies in your daily life. The solar transits also bring you creative energies that help you meet the goals you set for yourself each year.

The moon in Human Design represents the energy of what drives us. In traditional astrology, the new moon phase and the full moon phase represent bookend energies that mark the beginning and the end of a monthly creative cycle.

The new moon helps us set the intention for our goals for the month. The full moon supports us in releasing any energies, beliefs or blocks that are hindering the completion of our goals.

Lunar and solar eclipses are bookends that mark beginnings and endings. The work we do in between can be powerful, internal, as well as external. Eclipse energy represents cycles that support you in aligning more deeply with your bigger goals in life, as well as support you in breaking free from habits and patterns that keep you from growing and expanding.

To learn more about the transits and how they affect your personal Human Design chart and your energy click here:

http://www.freehumandesignchart.com

HOW TO USE THIS BOOK

The 2021 Quantum Human Design Evolution Guide is a workbook with a weekly writing assignment, affirmations, and Emotional Freedom Techniques (EFT) setup phrases. If you are not a fan of journaling, feel free to contemplate the prompts in whatever way works for you. You may walk with them, meditate on them or even discuss them with your friends.

This year I am excited to share with you updated Quantum Human Design language. Over the years it has become obvious to me the vocabulary in Human Design is in need of an upgrade in response to evolutionary shifts and with respect to new research that shows how the language we use is so powerful, it can even change your DNA. I hope you enjoy the new language!

Each of the Human Design Gates has a "challenge" associated with it. This is what you must master to get the most out of the movement of the Sun which occurs approximately every six days. Before you complete the writing assignment, read the "challenge" for each Gate and contemplate what you need to do to get the most out of each of the weekly archetypes.

The Emotional Freedom Techniques is a powerful energy psychology tool that has been scientifically proven to change your emotional, mental and genetic programming to help you express your highest potential. Each week you may work with a specific EFT setup phrase to help you clear any old energies you may be carrying related to the archetype of the week. (Learn more about how to use EFT here: www.quantumalignmentsystem.com/solar-transit- calendar)

You will also find exercises for each new moon, full moon, solar eclipse and lunar eclipse complete with a writing/contemplation assignment and affirmation. You'll be guided in working with the theme of the lunar cycles and eclipses so that you can make the most of these powerful energy cycles.

Every Human Design year gives us a 365-day creative cycle that supports us in releasing what no longer serves us, allows us to consciously increase our creative energy, grow, and evolve with the support of the stars.

May you have a prosperous and joyful 2021!

THE THEME OF THE YEAR:
2021 - The Year of Revolution and Reformation

I don't like starting my summary of the year ahead with a cautionary note, but I think it's vital that we enter the new year with the awareness that we are in the beginning of a revolution that started in late 2019 and promises to continue until 2024. Patience and the ability to sustain and endure are vital.

I want to gently remind you that the celestial weather and cycles of the next few years are bringing us essential energy to help us build an equitable, sustainable, and peaceful world. We can't *just* imagine and wish for a better world. We must do the inner and outer work of dismantling old structures, destroying outdated beliefs, and demolish the institutions and systems that no longer reflect our evolved understanding of the inherent value and beauty of all life on the planet.

Pluto continues to bless us with the theme of Truth this year. We are like Cosmic Spies of the Heart wearing powerful X-Ray glasses that allow us to see beyond the obvious and notice what patterns and Truths hide underneath. As lies, hidden agendas, dark drives, and motivations continue to be revealed alongside Truth, we will need to do the work to take down these old structures and begin the process of building something radically New.

We are learning to clear the inner effects of our conditioning that have clouded our vision. We are releasing old beliefs and seeing the truth behind the stories and myths we have embraced our entire lives, as a part of our old identities and as aspects of our cultural mythology. We are remembering our personal value, and this memory of the preciousness of who we truly are is helping us see the value in all people and, as such, the importance of all life.

2020 brought great chaos and confusion, but shock of 2020 is wearing off and we're beginning to understand that we are in a massive cycle of rebirth. We are not returning to the old ways. We are not who we used to be. We will have time to grieve along the way, but the planets are demanding we get to work!

The grieving process can feel unpredictable, emotional, and draining. We will need to factor in ways to process, integrate, and allow for self-compassion - and compassion for others - as we strengthen our endurance, access our sustainability, and cultivate perseverance.

We are consciously and deliberately crafting a new personal and collective narrative. This new narrative inspires us and calls us forth from the void we've been drifting in. We cannot afford to descend into the luxury of victimhood, blame, old patterns, or responses. This is powerful, transformative energy inviting us to find gratitude in the moment, to receive the lessons we've been given with grace, and to keep move forward.

We were born for this work.

We were born for this time.

It's time to face the painful consequences of our past actions and repay old debts, in order to stabilize our society and to rebuild with harmony. This is a powerful time of karmic alignment that calls for deep introspection and transparency. We must heal the trauma of the past to be able to realign with integrity and justice for all, so we may move forward with grace, clarity, and equality.

We are transforming our economy and reconciling our relationship with power and money. With a brand-new metric of value, we no longer measure value on the material plane, but instead, the currency of our new economy is discovering how we can amplify our well-being and use it to increase the quality of life and well-being for others.

We can no longer afford to see ourselves as separate from others. We are building a global and eco-centric economy. To take the first vital steps laying the foundation of a more equitable and sustainable world, we have to humbly admit that we are intricately and inextricably entangled with each other.

This year we begin to build a world filled with collaborative and co-creative possibility. Everything begins with self-responsibility. From a place of wholeness, we can enter into agreements without hidden agendas or the need to prove our value.

We must approach this year with the question: How can I best serve the world? Once we reclaim our value and gifts that only *we* can give the world, we can see our irreplaceable role in the cosmic plan and we can then commit to serving the world at our highest level because this place of service is also the place where we experience the deepest joy. This is the natural response to doing the inner work.

We are playing a long game. We must be patient and continue to keep the long-term vision in mind. We must remember to place our hands on each other's backs and ride the wave forward together. We will all win when we ALL win.

It will take tremendous courage this year to look at the dismantling and trust that, once we take things apart, there will be something better to build in its place. We must be willing to collaborate, explore, and experiment. We will be taking giant leaps of faith.

Our blessings this year will be amplified when we are willing to transform our old stories into a narrative that is truly worthy of who we are. We must trust our own intuitive awareness and be willing to do what feels right even if our logical, conditioned minds are fighting against what we once knew as "correct and aligned."

Faith stabilizes everything. Faith gives us the power to face potential emotional volatility and to trust that we can slice through the intensity bringing harmony to situations that feel unstable while we keep the "big picture" in mind. We must endure, even if we are in unfamiliar territory, questioning our definition of *momentum* and *progress*. Always trust that there is a bigger story unfolding.

We are on the cusp of a Creative Revolution that will, in time, be compared to the Scientific Revolution. We are on the edge of building the world we've been dreaming of since we were children. Innocence and joy are our key elements of creative power. It is from the playfulness of possibility thinking that the leading edge of a revolution and our evolution in consciousness will be advanced forward. We must act from the place of playfulness, believing—knowing—that evolution in consciousness will advance all of humanity forward.

2021 is the year we must do the inner work of clearing our old karma in order to be better able to translate Truth into action on the planet. Together, we will change the world, one shift in consciousness at a time. Once we make these vital shifts, the next right action steps will be revealed.

As always, take care of yourselves. Be generous to yourself and fill your own cup so that you have more to share. Trust in abundance and "enough-ness" and keep doing the right thing, even if you're—especially if you're—quaking in your boots.

From my Heart to Yours,

Karen

ECLIPSE SEASON

2021 arrives in the middle of an Eclipse Season that started on June 5, 2020 and will end on December 4, 2021. This eclipse season is on the Gemini/Sagittarius axis highlights two questions: How can we improve the way we transmit information, and how can we evolve it? Consider the following: traditional forms of education or school; the use of language; global relations (language, travel, communications); media and how it influences society; publishing; the role and function of law; social justice; and the role of religion.

Eclipse energy intensifies what is already happening on the planet. The theme of Eclipse season reverberates through all of the transits. Solar and Lunar Eclipses serve as a crucible of sorts, bringing the celestial themes into a catalytic state that amplifies the potential for growth and change.

Eclipses often bring us surprises, big twists in the plot line of our collective story and move us forward with a big "push", even when we think we're not ready (or we're resisting change). Eclipses highlight where we need to grow and add power to our evolutionary trajectory.

Eclipses always arrive in pairs, coinciding with new and full moons, as solar and lunar eclipses, respectively. They appear in a family of signs that are joined on the same axis. In other words, eclipse families come in pairs of signs that are found exactly opposite each other (six months apart) on the astrological wheel.

A solar eclipse occurs when the moon stands between the Sun and earth, cutting off the light of the Sun. This is what we typically think of when we use the word "eclipse," with the moon covering the Sun.

A lunar eclipse occurs when the earth stands between the moon and the Sun, cutting off the light of the Sun from the moon. The moon has no light of her own, as she simply reflects the light of the Sun. Here the moon basically disappears. A lunar eclipse is always a full moon and usually marks endings or culmination points.

Any eclipse is a significant event in the heavens. In truth, a solar eclipse is really a new moon on steroids and a lunar eclipse is a full moon on steroids – amplifying the strength of the moon's influence threefold or more.

Gemini energy brings the theme of communication. Sagittarius brings the theme of exploration and adventure. The two energies together invite us to explore our communication styles and how we can bring our communication into alignment with truth. We are learning how to share information with each other in spite of our differences. We're exploring how to use language to unify people around common ideas in order to collaborate and co-create in new ways.

Below is a list of all the Eclipse dates in this Eclipse cycle, including the Human Design Gates highlighted with each Eclipse:

June 5, 2020 - Lunar Eclipse in the Gate 35, the Gate of Experience

November 30, 2020 - Lunar Eclipse in the Gate 16, the Gate of Zest

December 14, 2020 - Solar Eclipse in the Gate 11, the Gate of the Conceptualist

May 26, 2021 - Lunar Eclipse in the Gate 34, the Gate of Power

June 10, 2021 - Solar Eclipse in the Gate 45, the Gate of Distribution

December 4, 2021 - Solar Eclipse in the Gate 5, the Gate of Consistency

You will find special Eclipse contemplations in the 2021 Evolution Guide inserted on the dates of the 2021 Eclipse events.

JANUARY 22, 2021

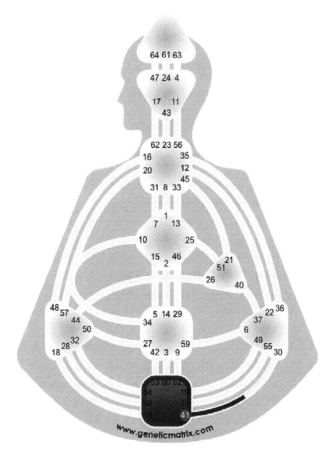

GATE 41: IMAGINATION

CHALLENGE:

To learn to use your imagination as a source of creative inspiration and manifestation. To experience the world and imagine more abundant possibilities. To stay connected to your creative fire.

JOURNAL QUESTIONS:

1. *Do I own my creative power? How can I deepen my self-honoring of my creative power?*

 ## AFFIRMATION:

I am a creative nexus of inspiration for the world. My ideas and imaginings inspire people to think beyond their limitations. My ideas stimulate new possibilities in the world. I am a powerful creator; my creative thoughts, ideas and inspirations set the stage for miracles and possibilities that will change the story of humanity.

 ## EFT SETUP:

Even though I'm afraid my dreams won't come true, I deeply and completely love and accept myself.

JANUARY 27, 2021

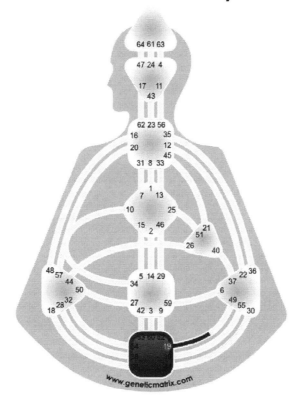

www.geneticmatrix.com

GATE 19: ATTUNEMENT

 CHALLENGE:

To learn how to manage being a highly sensitive person and not let your sensitivity cause you to compromise what you want and who you are. To learn to keep your own resources in a sustainable state in order so that you have more to give. To not martyr yourself to the needs of others. To learn how to become emotionally intimate without being shut down or co-dependent.

 JOURNAL QUESTIONS:

1. *Am I emotionally present in my relationships? Do I need to become more attuned to my own emotional needs and ask for more of what I want and need?*

 **AFFIRMATION:**

I am deeply aware of the emotional needs and energy of others. My sensitivity and awareness give me insights that allow me to create intimacy and vulnerability in my relationships. I am aware and attuned to the emotional frequency around me and I make adjustments to help support a high frequency of emotional alignment. I honor my own emotional needs as the foundation of what I share with others.

 EFT SETUP:

Even though it's scary to open my heart, I now choose to create space for deep intimacy and love in my life and I deeply and completely love and accept myself.

January 28, Full Moon

 Leo 9 degrees and 6 minutes

 Gate 33 - The Gate of Retelling

The Gate 33 brings us the lesson of learning to share our personal narrative in such a way that reflects our true value and our self-worth. When we share good stories about who we are, we not only set the tone and the direction for our own lives, we also show the way for others to improve their own life directions.

Challenge: Learn to share a personal narrative that reflects your true value and your worth. To share a personal narrative when it serves the intention of improving the direction of others. To share history in an empowering way.

Mastery: The ability to translate a personal experience into an empowering narrative that teaches and gives direction to others. Finding the power from the pain. Waiting for the right timing to transform or share a narrative so that it has the greatest impact on the Heart of another.

Unbalanced: Staying stuck and sharing a personal narrative rooted in pain, disempowerment and victimhood.

Writing Assignment: What personal narratives are you telling that might be keeping you stuck, feeling like a victim or feeling unlovable? How can you rewrite these stories?

What listening practices do you have? What can you do to listen better so that you can gauge when it is the right time to share in a powerful way?

Affirmation: I am a processor of stories. My gift is my ability to help others find the blessings, the love, and the power from stories of pain. I hold people's secrets and stories and transform them to share when the time is right. The stories I tell change the direction of people's lives. I use the power of stories to increase the power of Heart in the world and to help build a world of Love.

FEBRUARY 2, 2021

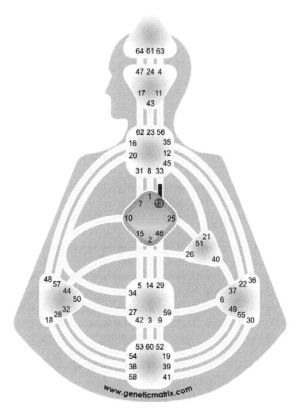

GATE 13: NARRATIVE

 ## CHALLENGE:

To forgive the past and redefine who you are each and every day. To tell a personal narrative that is empowering, self-loving and reflects your value and your authentic self. To bear witness to the pain and narrative of others and offer them a better story that allows them to expand on their abundance and blessings.

 ## JOURNAL QUESTIONS:

1. *What stories about my life am I holding on to?*

2. *Do these stories reflect who I really am and what I want to create in my life?*

3. *What or who do I need to forgive in order to liberate myself to tell a new story?*

4. *What secrets or stories am I holding for others? Do I need to release them?*

5. *Write the true story of who I really am….*

 # AFFIRMATION:

The story that I tell myself and the one I tell the world, sets the tone and direction for my life. I am the artist and creator of my story. I have the power to rewrite my story every day. The true story I tell from my Heart allows me to serve my Right Place in the Cosmic Plan.

 # EFT SETUP:

Even though I'm afraid to speak my truth, I now share the truth from my heart and trust that I am safe and I deeply and completely love and accept myself.

FEBRUARY 7, 2021

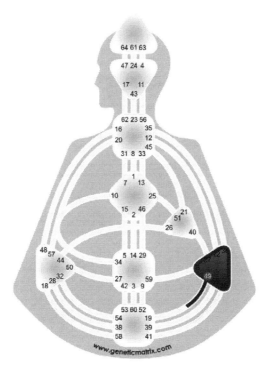

GATE 49: THE CATALYST

 CHALLENGE:

To not quit prematurely, failing to start a necessary revolution in your life, to not hold on to unhealthy situations, relationships or agreements that may compromise your value and worth.

 JOURNAL QUESTIONS:

1. *Am I holding on too long? Is there a circumstance and condition that I am allowing because I am afraid of the emotional energy associated with change?*

2. *Do I have a habit of quitting too soon? Do I fail to do the work associated with creating genuine intimacy?*

3. *What do I need to let go of right now to create room for me to align with higher principles?*

 **AFFIRMATION:**

I am a cosmic revolutionary. I am aligned with higher principles that support the evolution of humanity. I stand for peace, equity and sustainability. I align with these principles and I stand my ground. I do the work to create the intimacy necessary to share my values with others. I value myself and my work enough to only align with relationships that support my vital role.

 EFT SETUP:

Even though my emotional response causes me to react/paralyze me, I deeply and completely love and accept myself.

February 11, 2021 New Moon

 Aquarius 23 Degrees and 17 Minutes

 Gate 49 - The Gate of the Catalyst

New Moon energy invites us to explore how we can deepen our alignment with our intentions and asks us to focus on what we want to grow and expand on in our lives. The New Moon in the Gate 49, the Gate of Revolution, invites us to explore if it's time to release old circumstance and situations in our relationships that no longer serve us. Sometimes we hold on for too long and fail to start a "revolution" in our lives. Other times we quit too quickly and fail to see the results of continuing to refine and redefine intimacy.

This New Moon invites you to explore where you need to revolutionize your relationships, starting first with your relationship with yourself.

Challenge: To not quit prematurely and miss the opportunity to create intimacy. Or to hold on for longer than is healthy and to settle or compromise your value in situations, relationships, and with agreements that aren't worthy of you.

Mastery: The ability to sense when it's time to hold to principles that support your value. The ability to inspire others to make expansive changes that embrace higher principles and a deeper alignment with peace and sustainability. The willingness to align with a higher value. Knowing how to cultivate true intimacy in your relationships.

Unbalanced: Quitting too soon as a way of avoiding intimacy. Compromising on your value and upholding agreements that no longer serve you. Creating drama and fighting for outdated values that no longer serve the higher good.

Writing Assignment:

Where have you held on too long? What circumstances and/or conditions have you stayed in a relationship simply because you were afraid of the emotional energy of change?

What do you need to let go of right now to create room for you to align with higher principles?

Affirmation: I am a cosmic revolutionary. I am aligned with higher principles that support the evolution of humanity. I stand for peace, equity and sustainability. I align with these principles and I stand my ground. I do the work to create the intimacy necessary to share my values with others. I value myself and my work enough to only align with relationships that support my vital role.

FEBRUARY 13, 2021

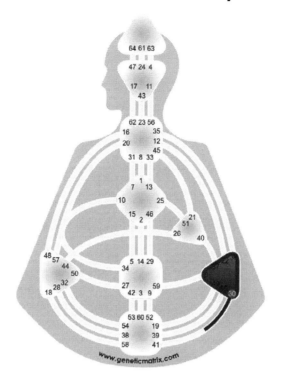

GATE 30: PASSION

CHALLENGE:

To be able to sustain a dream or a vision without burning out. To know which dream to be passionate about. To not let passion overwhelm you and to wait for the right timing to share your passion with the world.

JOURNAL QUESTIONS:

1. What am I passionate about? Have I lost my passion?

2. How is my energy? Am I physically burned out? Am I burned out on my idea?

3. What do I need to do to sustain my vision or dream about what I am inspired to create in my life?

4. Do I have a dream or vision I am avoiding because I'm afraid it won't come true?

 ## AFFIRMATION:

I am a passionate creator. I use the intensity of my passion to increase my emotional energy and sustain the power of my dream and what I imagine for Life. I trust in the Divine flow and I wait for the right timing and the right circumstances to act on my dream.

 ## EFT SETUP:

Even though my excitement feels like fear, I now choose to go forward with my passion on fire, fully trusting the infinite abundance of the Universe and I deeply and completely love and accept myself.

FEBRUARY 18, 2021

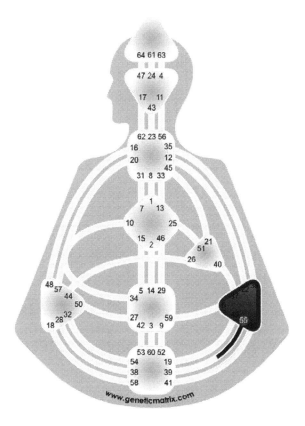

www.geneticmatrix.com

GATE 55: FAITH

 ## CHALLENGE:

To learn to trust Source. To know that you are fully supported. To master the art of emotional alignment AS your most creative power.

JOURNAL QUESTIONS:

1. *Do I trust that I am fully supported? What do I need to do to deepen that trust?*

2. *How can I align myself with abundant emotional energy? What practices or shifts do I need to make in my life to live and create in a more aligned way?*

3. *Do I surround myself with beauty? How can I deepen my experience of beauty in my life?*

4. *What do I have faith in now? What old gods of limitation do I need to stop worshipping?*

5. *Go on a miracle hunt. Take stock of everything good that has happened in my life. How much "magic" have I been blessed with?*

 ## AFFIRMATION:

I am perfectly and divinely supported. I know that all my needs and desires are being fulfilled. My trust in my support allows me to create beyond the limitation of what others think is possible and my faith shows them the way. I use my emotional energy as the source of my creative power. My frequency of faith lifts others up and opens up a greater world of potential and possibility.

 ## EFT SETUP:

Even though I struggle with faith and trusting Source, I deeply and completely love and accept myself.

FEBRUARY 24, 2021

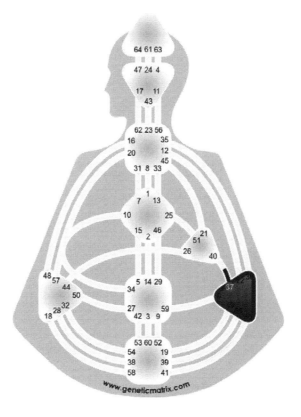

GATE 37: PEACE

 ## CHALLENGE:

To find inner peace as the true source to outer peace. To not let chaos and outer circumstances knock you off your center and disrupt your peace.

JOURNAL QUESTIONS:

1. *What habits, practices and routines do I have that cultivate my inner alignment with sustainable peace?*

2. *When I feel that my outer world is chaotic and disrupted how do I cultivate inner peace?*

3. *What do I need to do to cultivate a peaceful emotional frequency?*

 ## AFFIRMATION:

I am an agent of peace. My being, aligned with peace, creates an energy of contagious peace around me. I practice holding a peaceful frequency of energy and I respond to the world with an intention of creating sustainable peace.

 ## EFT SETUP:

Even though I struggle to create peace and harmony in my life, I deeply and completely love and accept myself.

February 27, 2021 Full Moon

 Virgo 8 Degrees and 57 Minutes

 Gate 40, The Gate of Restoration

Full moon energy invites us to explore what we need to release and let go of in order to stay in alignment with our intentions.

The Gate 40, the Gate of Restoration is an essential energy that helps us stay healthy and sustainable in the world. We need retreat, renewal, and rest to stay connected to our self-worth and to continue to act in integrity with ourselves and each other.

If we allow ourselves to become depleted, we lose our ability to do the work to sustain healthy agreements and contracts. We run the risk of pushing with energy we don't have and further depleting our reserves therefore putting us at risk for burnout.

This full moon invites you to let go of anything that is keeping you from nurturing yourself and getting the respite and renewal you need to be able to engage fully with your life.

Challenge: To learn to value yourself enough to retreat from community and the energy of those you love to restore, restock, and replenish your inner resources. To learn to interpret the signal of loneliness correctly. To take responsibility for your own care and resources and to not abdicate your own power to take care of yourself.

Mastery: The ability to retreat as a way of replenishing your inner and outer resources and to bring your renewed Self back into community when you are ready so that you have more to give.

Unbalanced: Martyrdom. Loneliness and blaming that causes you to compromise what you need and try to prove your value by overdoing and over-giving.

Writing Assignment:

What role does loneliness play in your life? Has loneliness caused you to doubt your value? What do you need to do to restore your energy? How do you take care of yourself? What agreements are you making in your relationships that might be causing you to compromise your value? How can you rewrite these agreements?

Are you abdicating your responsibility for your self-care? Are you living a "martyr" model?

What needs to be healed, released, aligned, and brought to your awareness for you to take responsibility for cultivating your own sense of value and self-worth?

Affirmation: I am a powerful resource for my community. The energy that I hold impacts others deeply and brings them to deeper states of alignment and sustainability. I take care of my body, mind, and soul because I know this: the more I am and the more that I have, the more I can give to others. I take care of myself first because I know that good things flow from me. I am valuable and powerful and I both claim and defend the true story of Who I Truly Am.

MARCH 2, 2021

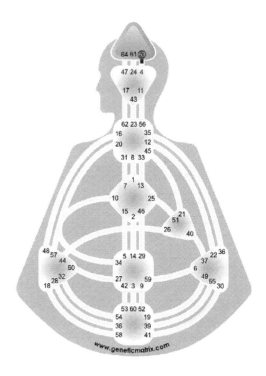

GATE 63: CURIOSITY

 CHALLENGE:

To not let self-doubt and suspicion cause you to stop being curious.

JOURNAL QUESTIONS:

1. *Am I curious about life? Do I regularly allow myself to be curious about what else is possible in the world? In my life?*

2. *Do I doubt myself and my ideas?*

3. *What needs to happen for me to unlock my need to be right about an idea and to allow myself to dream of possibilities again?*

 ## AFFIRMATION:

My curiosity makes me a conduit of possibility thinking. I ask questions that stimulate imaginations. I allow the questions of my mind to seed dreams that stimulate my imagination and the imagination of others. I share my questions as an opening to the fulfillment of potential in the world.

 ## EFT SETUP:

Even though I struggle with trusting myself, I now choose to relax and know that I know. I listen to my intuition. I abandon logic and let my Higher Knowing anchor my spirit in trust, and I deeply and completely love and accept myself.

MARCH 7, 2021

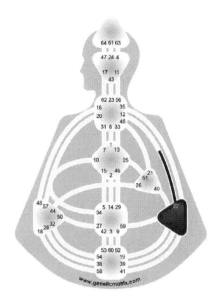

GATE 22: SURRENDER

 **CHALLENGE:**

To trust that your passions and deepest desires are supported by the Universal flow of abundance. To have the courage to follow your passion and know that you'll be supported. To learn to regulate your emotional energy so that you have faith that everything will unfold perfectly.

 JOURNAL QUESTIONS:

1. *Where am I denying my passion in my life? Where have I settled for less than what I want because I'm afraid I can't get what I want?*

2. *What do I need to do to fully activate my passion? What is one bold step towards my genius that I could take right now?*

3. *Do I trust the Universe? What do I need to do to deepen my trust?*

4. *Do I have a regular practice that supports me in sustaining a high frequency of emotional energy and alignment?*

5. *What needs to be healed, released, aligned and brought to my awareness for me to deepen my faith?*

 ## AFFIRMATION:

I am a global change agent. I am inspired with passions that serve the purpose of transforming the world. I trust that my emotions and my passion will align me with faith and the flow of resources I need to do to fulfill my life purpose. When I let go and follow my passion, I am given everything I need to change the world.

 ## EFT SETUP:

Even though it's hard to trust in my support, I now choose to trust anyway and I deeply and completely love and accept myself.

MARCH 13, 2021

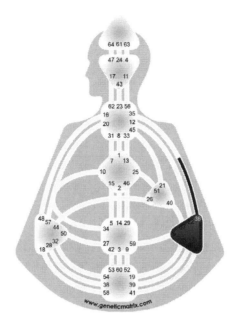

GATE 36: EXPLORATION

CHALLENGE:

To not let boredom cause you to leap into chaos. To learn to stick with something long enough to become masterful and to bear the fruits of your experience.

JOURNAL QUESTIONS:

1. *How does boredom impact my life? What do I do when I feel bored? What can I do to keep myself aligned even when I'm bored?*

2. *What stories have I experienced that have shattered old patterns and expectations? How have my stories changed or inspired others?*

3. *What do I do to maintain or sustain emotional alignment? What do I need to add to my daily practice to "amp" up my emotional energy around my intentions?*

 ## AFFIRMATION:

My experiences and stories break old patterns and push the boundaries of the edge of what's possible for humanity. I defy the patterns and I create miracles through my emotional alignment with possibility. I hold my vision and maintain my emotional energy as I wait to bear the fruit of my intentions and my visions.

 ## EFT SETUP:

Even though it's scary to be out of my comfort zone, I now choose to push myself into something new and more aligned with my Truth and I deeply and completely love and accept myself.

March 13, 2021 - New Moon

 **Pisces 23 degrees and 4 minutes**

 Gate 36, The Gate of Exploration

New Moon energy invites us to explore how we can deepen our alignment with our intentions and asks us to focus on what we want to grow and expand on in our lives. The Gate 36, the Gate of Exploration, invites us to look at where we need to break free from patterns of the past and start something new. This New Moon is encouraging you to explore what you really want in your life and to begin to take the actions necessary to break free from old patterns that might be keeping you stuck or bored with your life.

The theme of creating something new and different mixed with New Moon energy gives us a powerful theme of initiating change in our lives. The potential for creating miracles lives in this Gate. The only thing that can limit us is our resistance to letting go of the patterns of the past. Don't worry about "how" your desires can manifest. Simply hold the intention and wait and see what shows up!

Challenge: To not let boredom cause you to leap into chaos. To learn to stick with something long enough to become masterful and to bear the fruits of your experience.

Mastery: The ability to hold a vision and sustain it with an aligned frequency of emotional energy and to bring the vision into form when the timing is right. The ability to stretch the boundaries of the story of Humanity by breaking patterns. Creating miracles through emotional alignment.

Unbalanced: Not waiting for the right timing and leaping into new opportunities without waiting for alignment, causing chaos. Leaping from opportunity to opportunity without waiting to see how the story will play out and never getting to experience the full fruition of the experience.

Writing Assignment:

How does boredom impact your life? What do you do when you feel bored? What can you do to keep yourself aligned even when you're bored?

What stories have you experienced that have shattered old patterns and expectations? How have your stories changed or inspired others?

What do you do to maintain or sustain emotional alignment? What do you need to add to your daily practice to "amp" up your emotional energy around your intentions?

Affirmation: My experiences and stories break old patterns and push the boundaries of the edge of what's possible for humanity. I defy the patterns and I create miracles through my emotional alignment with possibility. I hold my vision and maintain my emotional energy as I wait to bear the fruit of my intentions and my visions.

MARCH 19, 2021

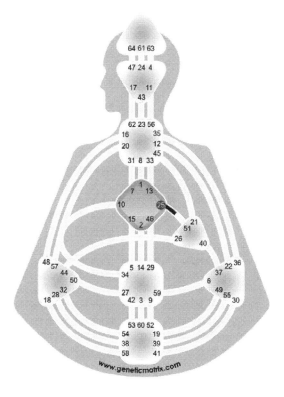

GATE 25: SPIRIT

 ## CHALLENGE:

To trust the Divine Order in all of your life. To learn to connect with Source as the path to creating well-being in your life. To remember that your life serves an irreplaceable role in the cosmic plan and to honor that role and to live from it. To trust Source.

JOURNAL QUESTIONS:

1. *Do I trust Source?*

2. *Do I have a regular practice that connects me to Source?*

3. *Do I know my Life Purpose? Am I living true to my Purpose? How can I deepen my connection to my Purpose?*

 **AFFIRMATION:**

I am an agent of the Divine. My life is the fulfillment of Divine Order and the Cosmic Plan. When I am connected to Source, I serve my right place. I take up no more than my space and no less than my place in the world. I serve and through serving, I am supported.

 EFT SETUP:

Even though in the past, I was afraid to follow my heart, I now choose to do what is right for me and know that I am fully supported and I deeply and completely love and accept myself.

MARCH 24, 2021

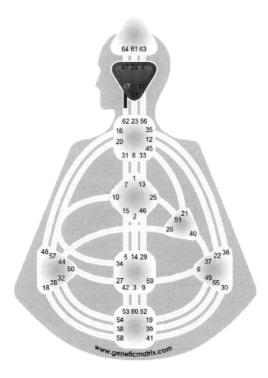

www.geneticmatrix.com

GATE 17: ANTICIPATION

 ## CHALLENGE:

To learn to share your thoughts about possibilities only when people ask for them. To not let doubt and suspicion keep you from seeing the potential of positive outcomes.

JOURNAL QUESTIONS:

1. *What do I need to do to manage my insights and ideas so that they increase the options and potential of others?*

2. *How do I feel about holding back from sharing my insights until the timing is right? What can I do to manage my need to share without waiting for the right timing?*

3. *What routines and strategies do I need to cultivate to keep my perspectives expanding and possibility oriented?*

4. *How can I improve my ability to manage doubt and fear?*

AFFIRMATION:

I use the power of my mind to explore possibilities and potential. I know that the inspirations and insights that I have create exploration and experimentation that can inspire the elegant solutions necessary to master the challenges facing humanity.

EFT SETUP:

Even though I have a lot of ideas and thoughts to share, I trust that the insights that I have to offer are too important to blurt out and I wait for the right people to ask and I deeply and completely love and accept myself.

March 28, 2021 - Full Moon

 Libra 8 degrees 18 minutes

 Gate 18, The Gate of Re-Alignment

Full moon energy invites us to explore what we need to release in order to stay in alignment with our intentions.

The Gate 18, the Gate of Re-Alignment is a powerful energy that brings correction to mis-aligned patterns. This energy can often feel like criticism, but the true purpose of this Gate is to support us in releasing patterns that keep us from experiencing true joy.

This full moon invites you to release any old patterns that are keeping you from experiencing joy in your life and encourages you to make the changes necessary to make joy and joyful living a priority.

This energy is intended for us to focus inward on ourselves. When this energy is featured in the Cosmic Weather, it can often feel like others are criticizing us or we can feel critical of others. There can be deep wisdom in the re-alignment we receive from others. Try to listen and receive without feeling hurt. It's also essential that we ask before we share our own insights into how others can create and experience deeper states of joy.

Be gentle with your words when this energy is at play!

Challenge: To learn to wait for the right timing and the right circumstances to offer your intuitive insights into how to fix or correct a pattern. To wait for the right time and the right reason to share your critique. To understand that the purpose of re-alignment is to create more joy, not to be "right".

Mastery: To see a pattern that needs correcting and to wait for the right timing and circumstances to correct and align it. To serve joy.

Unbalanced: To be critical. To share criticism without respect for the impact. To be more concerned with your own "rightness" than to assess whether your insight is actually adding to more joy in the world.

Writing Assignment:

What does joy mean to you? How do you serve it?

How do you cultivate joy in your own life?

How does it feel to be "right" about something and keep it to yourself? Do you need to release any old "stories" about needing to be "right"?

Do you trust your own insights? Do you have the courage to share them when it's necessary?

Affirmation: I am a powerful force that re-aligns patterns. My insights and awareness give people the information they need to deepen their mastery and to experience greater joy. I serve joy and I align the patterns of the world to increase the world's potential for living in the flow of joy.

MARCH 30, 2021

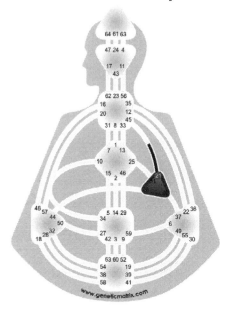

GATE 21: SELF-REGULATION

 ## CHALLENGE:

To learn to let go. To master self-regulation. To release the need to control others and circumstances. To trust in the Divine and to know that you are supported. Knowing that you are worthy of support and you don't have to over-compensate.

JOURNAL QUESTIONS:

1. *Where do I need to release control in my life?*

2. *Do I trust the Universe?*

3. *Do I value myself? Do I trust that I'll be supported in accordance with my value?*

4. *What do I need to do to create an internal and external environment of self- generosity?*

5. *What needs to be healed, released, aligned and brought to my awareness for me to embrace my true value?*

 ## AFFIRMATION:

I am worthy of claiming, protecting and defending my rightful place in the world. I create an inner and outer environment that is self-generous and I regulate my environment to sustain a high frequency of alignment with my true value. I know that I am an irreplaceable and precious part of the cosmic plan and I create my life to reflect the importance of my right place in the world.

 ## EFT SETUP:

Even though in the past I felt like I had to control everything, I now surrender to Source and know that my abundance, my TRUE abundance, is available to me when I let go and let the Universe do the work and I deeply and completely love and accept myself.

APRIL 5, 2021

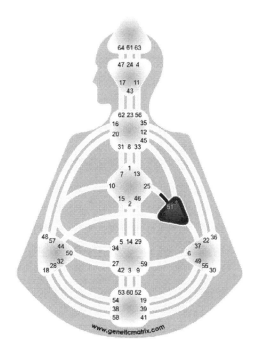

GATE 51: INITIATION

 ## CHALLENGE:

To not let the unexpected cause you to lose your faith. To not let a pattern of unexpected events cause you to lose your connection with your purpose and Source. To learn to use the power of your own story of initiation to initiate others into fulfilling their rightful place in the Cosmic Plan.

JOURNAL QUESTIONS:

1. *What has shock and the unexpected taught me in my life?*

2. *How can I deepen my connection to Source?*

3. *How can my experiences of initiation be shared with others? What am I here to "wake people up" to?*

 # AFFIRMATION:

I navigate change and transformation with Grace. I know that when my life takes a twist or a turn, it is my soul calling me out to serve at a higher level. I use disruption as a catalyst for my own growth and expansion. I am a teacher and an initiator. I use my ability to transform pain into growth and power to help others navigate through crisis and emerge on the other side of crisis empowered and aligned.

 # EFT SETUP:

Even though things aren't turning out like I expected, I now choose to embrace the unexpected and trust that the Universe is always serving my Greater Good and I deeply and completely love and accept myself.

APRIL 10, 2021

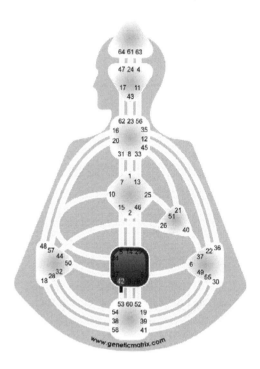

GATE 42: CONCLUSION

 ## CHALLENGE:

To learn to bring things to completion. To allow yourself to be led to where you need to be to finish things. To value your ability to know how to finish and to learn to give up your need to try to start everything. To finish things in order to create space for something new.

JOURNAL QUESTIONS:

1. *Do I own and value my natural gift of knowing how to bring things to completion?*

2. *What things in my life do I need to finish in order to make room for something new?*

3. *Am I holding on to old circumstances and patterns because I'm afraid to let them go?*

4. *Do I judge myself for "not starting things"? How can I learn to be gentler with myself?*

 **AFFIRMATION:**

I am gifted at knowing when and how to finish things. I respond to bringing events, experiences and relationships to a conclusion in order to create space for something new and more abundant. I can untangle the cosmic entanglements that keep people stuck in old patterns. My ability to re-align and complete things helps others create space for transformation and expansion.

 EFT SETUP:

Even though I've hesitated in the past to finish what I needed to finish in order to make room for something new and better, I now choose to bring things to a powerful ending. I know that I am taking strong action to create space for what I truly want to create in my life and I deeply and completely love myself.

April 12, 2021 - New Moon

 **Aries 22 degrees 25 minutes**

 Gate 42, The Gate of Conclusion

New Moon energy invites us to explore how we can deepen our alignment with our intentions and asks us to focus on what we want to grow and expand on in our lives. The New Moon in the Gate 42, the Gate of Conclusion, brings us an interesting conundrum. The New Moon pushes on us and begs us to start something new, while the Gate 42 invites us to finish things up and to bring things to a conclusion. This New Moon energy invites us to explore what we need to finish up and move out of the way in order to make room for something better. This is "spring cleaning" energy that encourages us to open up space, get things in order, and finish the things that have been depleting us or distracting us from doing what we really desire to do with our lives.

The Gate 42 is one of the Gates that contains the "code" for influencing Divine Timing. If you're feeling stuck or like things aren't happening at the speed that you were hoping for, it's often because there isn't "room" for something new in your life. When we remove old situations, beliefs, and patterns, clearing the way to create space, the Universe often responds in kind by bringing us something better - something more in alignment with what we really want.

Be mindful with this energy. Remove things with great deliberation and intention. You are welcoming in the new, not destroying and fighting the old.

Challenge: To learn to bring things to completion. To allow yourself to be led to where you need to be to finish things. To value your ability to know how to finish and to learn to give up your need to try to start everything. To finish things in order to create space for something new.

Mastery: The ability to respond to being inserted into opportunities, experiences, and events that you have the wisdom to facilitate and complete. To know exactly what needs to be completed in order to create the space for something new.

Unbalanced: Pressure, confusion, and self-judgement for not being able to get things started. Avoiding or putting off things that need to be completed creating a backlog of projects that can lead to paralysis and overwhelm. Finishing things prematurely due to pressure.

Writing Assignment:

What is your experience with completion?

What things in your life do you need to finish in order to make room for something new?

What patterns or circumstances do you hold on to because you fear letting them go?

Do you judge yourself for "not starting things"? How can you learn to be gentler with yourself?

Affirmation: I am gifted at knowing when and how to finish things. I respond to bringing events, experiences, and relationships to conclusion in order to create space for something new and more abundant. I can maneuver through the cosmic entanglements that keep people stuck in old patterns. My ability to re-align and complete things helps others create space for transformation and expansion.

APRIL 16, 2021

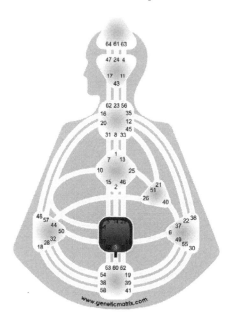

GATE 3: INNOVATION

CHALLENGE:

To learn to trust in Divine Timing and to know that your ideas and insights will be transmitted to the world when the world is ready.

JOURNAL QUESTIONS:

1. *Where has Divine Timing worked out in my life? What has waiting taught me?*

2. *Do I trust in Divine Timing?*

3. *If the opportunity to share my ideas with the world presented itself today, would I be ready? If not, what do I need to prepare to be ready?*

AFFIRMATION:

I am here to bring change to the world. My natural ability to see what else is possible to create something new is my strength and my gift. I patiently cultivate my inspiration and use my understanding of what is needed to help evolve the world.

 ## EFT SETUP:

Even though it's scary to take the first step, I now trust the Universe and my ability to be innovative and know that I stand on the cusp of the fulfillment of my Big Dreams. I deeply and completely love and accept myself.

APRIL 22, 2021

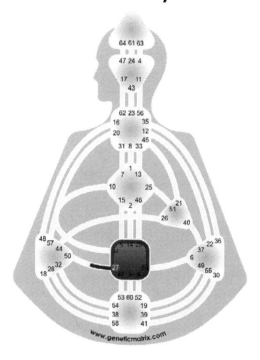

GATE 27: ACCOUNTABILITY

 CHALLENGE:

To care without over-caring. To allow others to assume responsibility for their own challenges and choices. To learn to accept other people's values. To not let guilt cause you to compromise what is good and right for you.

JOURNAL QUESTIONS:

1. *Am I taking responsibility for things that aren't mine to be responsible for? Whose problem is it? Can I return the responsibility for the problem back to its rightful owner?*

2. *What role does guilt play in motivating me? Can I let go of the guilt? What different choices might I make if I didn't feel guilty?*

3. *What obligations do I need to set down in order for me to take better care of myself?*

4. *Are there places where I need to soften my judgements of other people's values?*

 ## AFFIRMATION:

I have a nurturing and loving nature. It is my gift to be able to love and care for others. I know that the greatest expression of my love is to treat others as capable and powerful. I support when necessary and I let go with love so my loved ones can discover their own strength and power.

 ## EFT SETUP:

Even though it's hard to say no, I now choose to take the actions that are correct for me. I release my guilt and I deeply and completely love and accept myself.

April 27, 2021 - Full Moon

 Scorpio 7 degrees 6 minutes

 Gate 28 - The Gate of Adventure and Challenge

Full moon energy invites us to explore what we need to release and let go of in order to stay in alignment with our intentions.

The Gate 28 invites us to release where we've let the fear of things being too difficult, meaningless or too challenging stops us from fulfilling our dream. The Gate 28 invites us to release the fear of things being too meaningless or too challenging. Each of these stops us from fulfilling our dreams.

The Gate 28 teaches us what is really worth fighting for and pushing towards. The challenges we face forge our strength and serve to deepen our conviction and our willingness to do take actions that bring us into a deeper state of alignment with transformation, evolution, and growth.

It is also a "fear" Gate of the Spleen Center that can leave us paralyzed in inaction if we think the challenge ahead will be difficult. This Full Moon encourages us to explore how we are using our energy and to discern where we choose to place our focus and drive.

Challenge: To not let struggle and challenge leave you feeling defeated and despairing. To learn to face life as an adventure. Do not let challenge and struggle cause you to feel as if you have failed.

Mastery: To learn to share from your personal experience, your struggles, and your triumphs. To persevere and to know that your adventures deepen your ability to transform life into a meaningful journey. To understand that your struggles help deepen the collective ideas about what is truly valuable and worthy of creating.

Unbalanced: Refusing to take action out of fear that the journey will be too painful, too difficult, or even impossible. To feel like a failure. To fall into victim consciousness.

Writing Assignment:

How can you turn your challenge into adventure?

Where do you need to cultivate a sense of adventure in your life?

What do you need to do to rewrite the story of your "failures"?

What meanings, blessings and lessons have you learned from your challenges?

What needs to be healed, released, aligned and brought to your awareness for you to trust yourself and your choices?

What do you need to do to forgive yourself for your perceived past failures?

Affirmation: I am here to push the boundaries of life and what is possible. I thrive in situations that challenge me. I am an explorer on the leading edge of consciousness and my job is to test how far I can go. I embrace challenge. I am an adventurer. I share all that I have learned from my challenges with the world. My stories help give people greater meaning, teach them what is truly worthy of creating, and inspire people to transform.

APRIL 28, 2021

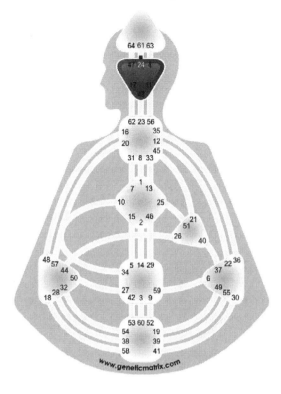

GATE 24: BLESSINGS

 CHALLENGE:

To learn to allow what you truly deserve in your life. To not rationalize an experience that allowed for less than you deserve. To find the blessings and power from painful experiences and to use them as catalysts for transformation.

JOURNAL QUESTIONS:

1. What are the blessings I learned from my greatest painful experiences? Can I see how these experiences served to teach me? What did I learn?

2. What am I grateful for from the past?

3. Where might I be rationalizing staying stuck or settling for less than what I really want or deserve? What do I need to do to break out of this pattern?

 **AFFIRMATION:**

I embrace the Mystery of Life with the awareness that the infinite generosity of the Universe gives me blessings in every event in my life. I find the blessings from the pain. I grow and expand beyond the limitations of my experiences and stories. I use what I have learned to create a life and circumstances that reflect the miracle that I am.

 EFT SETUP:

Even though it's scary to start something new...I'm afraid I'm not ready...I now choose to courageously embrace the new and trust that everything is in Divine Order and I deeply and completely love and accept myself.

MAY 3, 2021

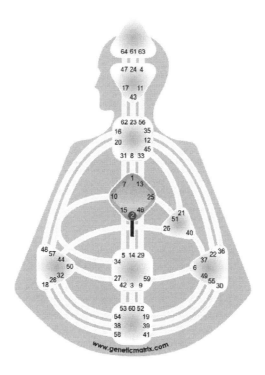

GATE 2: ALLOWING

 CHALLENGE:

To love yourself enough to open to the flow of support, love and abundance. To incrementally increase over the course of your life what you're willing to allow yourself to receive. To learn to know that you are valuable and lovable simply because you exist.

 JOURNAL QUESTIONS:

1. *Do I ask for help when I need it? Why or why not?*

2. *Do I trust the Universe/God/Spirit/Source to support me in fulfilling my intentions?*

3. *Am I grateful for what I have? Make a list of everything I'm grateful for.*

4. *Can I transform my worry into trust?*

5. *Do I believe that I deserve to be supported?*

AFFIRMATION:

I allow myself to receive the full flow of resources and abundance I need to fully express all of who I am. I recognize that my life is a vital, irreplaceable part of the cosmic tapestry and I receive all that I need because it helps me contribute all that I am.

 ## EFT SETUP:

Even though I'm scared because nothing looks like I thought it would, I now choose to relax, trust and receive the support that I am designed to receive. I know that I will be supported in expressing my True Self and I deeply and completely love and accept myself.

MAY 9, 2021

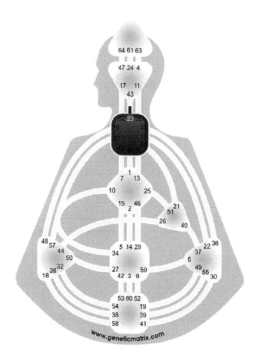

GATE 23: TRANSMISSION

CHALLENGE:

To recognize that change and transformation are inevitable. To know what needs to happen next, to wait for the right timing and the right people to share your insights with. To not jump the gun and try to convince people to understand what you know. To not let yourself slip into negativity and despair when people aren't ready.

JOURNAL QUESTIONS:

1. *How can I strengthen my connection to Source?*

2. *Do I trust what I know? What comes up for me when I know something but I don't know how I know what I know?*

3. *How do I handle myself when I know something but the people around me aren't ready to hear it yet?*

AFFIRMATION:

I change the world with what I know. My insights and awarenesses have the ability to transform the way people think and perceive the world. I know that my words are powerful and transformative. I trust that the people who are ready for the change that I bring will ask me for what I know. I am a vessel for my knowingness and I nurture myself while I wait to share what I know.

 EFT SETUP:

Even though in the past I shut down my voice, I now speak my truth and offer the contribution of my unique spirit to the world and I deeply and completely love and accept myself.

May 11, 2021 - New Moon

 Taurus 21 degrees 18 minutes

 Gate 23 - The Gate of Transmission

New Moon energy invites us to explore how we can deepen our alignment with our intentions and asks us to focus on what we want to grow and expand on in our lives. The Gate 23 brings us the energy of being able to translate what we know into words and ultimately, action. This is the energy of change and transformation. We are changing the way we think and the ideas that we hold have the power to transform the way others see the world and understand information.

The Gate 23 is "knowingness", a deep connection to our understanding of Truth. We know and trust what we know when we deepen our connection Source. We can't trust what we know if we don't trust Source.

The Gate 23 brings us the energy of something new. This New Moon invites us to set intentions that support us in expressing our insights and new ideas while transforming our old thought patterns and understandings. It's a great New Moon to help you share your new ideas with the world.

Challenge: To recognize that change and transformation are inevitable. To know what needs to happen next and to have to wait for the right timing and the right people with whom to share your insights. To practice patience and try not to convince people to understand what you know. To not let yourself slip into negativity and despair when people aren't ready.

Mastery: The ability to be able to translate insights for people that offer a way to transform how they think. To share what you know with awareness of right timing, and to trust your knowingness as an expression of your connection to Source.

Unbalanced: The need to be right. An anxiety or pressure to share what you know with people who aren't ready and then to feel despair or bitterness that they don't understand things the way you do.

Writing Assignment:
How can you strengthen your connection to Source?
Do you trust what you know? What comes up for you when you "know" something but you don't know how you know what you know?
How do you handle yourself when you know something but the people around you aren't ready to hear it yet?

Affirmation: I change the world with what I know. My insights and knowledge have the ability to transform the way people think and perceive the world. I know that my words are powerful and transformative. I trust that the people who are ready for the change that I bring will ask me for what I know. I am a vessel for my knowingness and I nurture myself while I wait to share what I know.

MAY 15, 2021

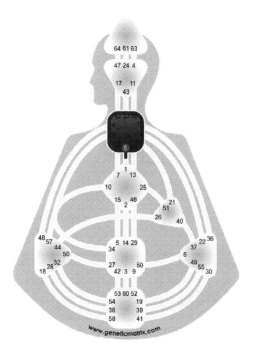

GATE 8: FULFILLMENT

 ## CHALLENGE:

The learn to express yourself authentically. To wait for the right people to see the value of who you are and to share yourself with them, with vulnerability and all of your heart. To learn to trust that you are a unique expression of the Divine with a purpose and a path. To find that path and to walk it without self-judgement or holding back.

JOURNAL QUESTIONS:

1. *Do I feel safe being vulnerable? What experiences have caused me to feel unsafe expressing my true self? Can I rewrite those stories?*

2. *What would an uncompromising life look like for me?*

3. *What do I need to remove from my current life to make my life more authentic?*

4. *What is one bold action I can take right now that would allow me to express who I am more authentically in the world? What is my true passion? What do I dream of?*

 **AFFIRMATION:**

I am devoted to the full expression of who I am. I defend and protect the story of my Life. I know that when I am expressing myself, without hesitation or limitation, I AM the contribution that I am here to give the world. Being myself IS my life purpose and my direction flows from my authentic alignment.

 EFT SETUP:

Even though I question whether I have something of value to add to the world, I now choose to courageously follow the whispers of my soul and live a life that is a powerful expression of the truth of who I am. I speak my truth. I value my contribution. I know I am precious and I deeply and completely love and accept myself.

MAY 21, 2021

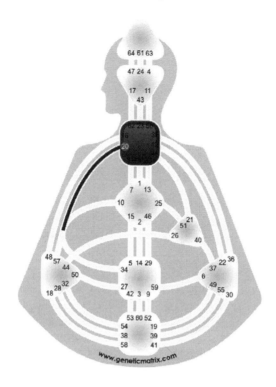

GATE 20: PATIENCE

 ## CHALLENGE:

To be patient and master the ability to wait. To be prepared and watchful but resist the urge to act if the timing isn't right or if there are details that still need to be readied.

 ## JOURNAL QUESTIONS:

1. *How do I manage my need for action? Am I patient? Do I trust in Divine Timing?*

2. *Do I trust my intuition?*

3. *What needs to be healed, released, aligned and brought to my awareness for me to trust my intuition?*

4. *What needs to be healed, released, aligned and brought to my awareness for me to trust my intuition?*

AFFIRMATION:

I am in the flow of perfect timing. I listen to my intuition. I prepare. I gather the experience, resources and people I need to support my ideas and my principles. When I am ready, I wait patiently, knowing that right timing is the key to transforming the world. My alignment with right timing increases my influence and my power.

EFT SETUP:

Even though it's scary to not **do** anything and wait, I now choose to trust the infinite abundance of the Universe and I deeply and completely love and accept myself.

May 26, 2021 Total Lunar Eclipse and Full Moon

 Sagittarius 5 degrees and 26 minutes

 Gate 34 - The Gate of Power

Full moon energy invites us to explore what we need to release and let go of in order to stay in alignment with our intentions. Eclipse energy amplifies the intensity of the Full Moon.

This powerful Full Moon Eclipse brings us the theme of power.

We are being invited to explore what stands in our way, keeping us from feeling powerful or trapping us in our powerlessness.

The Gate 34, the most powerful Gate on the Human Design chart, is rooted on the Sacral Center. The Sacral Center is responsive. This Gate teaches us that we are the most powerful when we respond, setting us to learn the difference between power and force.

You cannot force power. True power lies in the ability to respond to the needs of the planet, and the needs of others, and then to unify people around common ideas that create sustainability in the world. This is the power of true caring and nurturing in its highest expression.

The challenge Gate 34 brings is trusting and waiting in Divine Timing and the importance of being ready when the time to respond is at hand. This Full Moon invites you to explore what you need to do to sustain your energy so that you can tap into your true power when the timing is right.

Challenge: To learn to measure energy in order to stay occupied and busy, but not to burn yourself out trying to force the timing or the "rightness" of a project. To wait to know which project or creation to implement based on when you get something to respond to.

Mastery: The ability to respond to opportunities to unify the right people around a transformative and powerful idea when the timing and circumstances are correct.

Unbalanced: Being too busy to tune into the right timing and the right people. Feeling frustrated with pushing and "trying" to make things happen. Forcing manifestation with little results. Depleting yourself because you're pushing too hard.

Writing Assignment:
Do you trust in Divine Timing? What do you need to do to deepen your trust?
How do you cultivate greater patience in your life?
What fears come up for you when you think of waiting? How can you learn to wait with greater faith and ease?
What do you do to occupy yourself while you're waiting?

Affirmation:
I am a powerful servant of Divine Timing. When the timing is right, I unify the right people around the right idea, and create transformation on the planet. My power is more active when I allow the Universe to set the timing. I wait. I am patient. I trust.

MAY 27, 2021

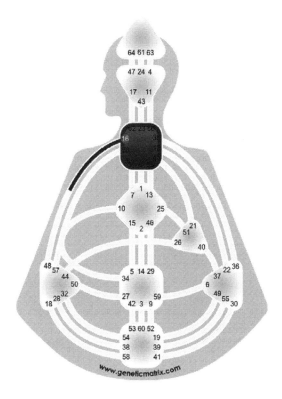

GATE 16: ZEST

 CHALLENGE:

To learn to temper your enthusiasm by making sure you're prepared enough for whatever it is you're trying to do or create.

JOURNAL QUESTIONS:

1. *Do I trust my gut?*

1. *Do I need to slow down and make sure I've done my homework before I take action?*

1. *Have I sidelined my enthusiasm because other people have told me that I can't do what I'm dreaming of doing?*

 **AFFIRMATION:**

I am a faith-filled contagious force. I take guided actions and I trust my intuition and awareness to let me know when I am prepared and ready to leap into expanding my experience and mastery. My enthusiasm inspires others to trust in themselves and to take their own giant leaps of growth.

 EFT SETUP:

Even though I'm afraid that I'm not fulfilling my life purpose and I'm wasting my life, I now choose to relax and know that I am in the perfect place at the perfect time to fulfill my destiny and I deeply and completely love and accept myself.

JUNE 2, 2021

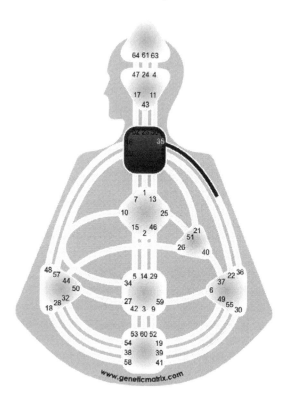

GATE 35: EXPERIENCE

 CHALLENGE:

To not let experience lead to feeling jaded or bored. To have the courage to share what you know from your experience. To know which experiences are worth participating in. To let your natural ability to master anything keep you from being enthusiastic about learning something new. To embrace that even though you know how to know, you don't know everything.

JOURNAL QUESTIONS:

1. *Where am I finding passion in my life? Do I need to create or discover more passion in my life right now?*

2. *Do I share my knowledge and the stories of my experiences? Do I see the value of what I have to share?*

3. *What am I curious about? How can I expand on that curiosity?*

AFFIRMATION:

I am an experienced, wise and knowledgeable resource for others. My experiences in life have added to the rich tapestry that is the story of Humanity. I share my stories with others because my experiences open doorways of possibility for others. My stories help others create miracles in their lives.

 ## EFT SETUP:

Even though in the past I struggled to stay focused and move forward, I now trust myself to take the next steps on manifesting my dream. I am focused, clear and moving forward and I deeply and completely love and accept myself.

JUNE 7, 2021

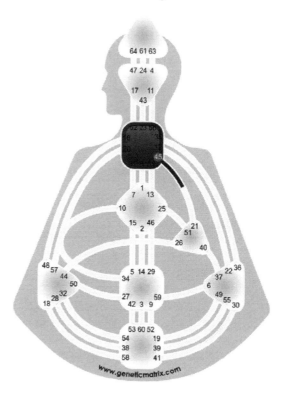

GATE 45: DISTRIBUTION

 ## CHALLENGE:

To share and use your resources for the greater good of the whole. To learn to manage resources judiciously so that they benefit the most amount of people. To teach as a pathway of sharing.

JOURNAL QUESTIONS:

1. *Do I like to share? What do I have to give the world?*

2. *How do I own my right leadership? Am I comfortable as a leader? Do I shrink from leadership? Do I overcompensate by pushing too hard with my leadership?*

3. *Do I trust that when the right people are ready I will be pressed into action as a leader and a teacher? What do I need to heal, release, align or bring to my awareness to trust my leadership energy more?*

 **AFFIRMATION:**

I am a teacher and a leader. I use my resources, my knowledge and my experience to expand the resources, knowledge and experiences of others. I use my blessings of abundance to increase the blessings of others. I know that I am a vehicle of wisdom and knowledge. I sense when it's right for me to share who I am and what I know with others.

 EFT SETUP:

Even though I'm afraid to look at my finances, I now choose to take a real look at my financial numbers and know that awareness is the first step to increasing my financial status and I deeply and completely love and accept myself.

June 10, 2021 - Annular Solar Eclipse and New Moon

 Gemini 19 degrees and 42 minutes

 Gate 45 - The Gate of Distribution

New Moon energy invites us to explore how we can deepen our alignment with our intentions and asks us to focus on what we want to grow and expand on in our lives. Eclipse energy amplifies the intensity of the New Moon.

The Gate 45, one of the teaching gates, gives us the energy to share. We are invited to explore what we have to give to each other and to the world with this powerful celestial weather.

The Gate 45 is an extension of the Will Center, the Center that holds our energy for our self-worth and our perception of our value in the world. We can only give if we, ourselves, have enough and perceive ourselves as being enough. This eclipse, along with the new moon, encourages you to first nurture yourself so that you can sustainably share yourself with the world.

This is a powerful time to begin the process of sharing your Heart with the world. It takes courage to show the world the heart of who you are. It is from the authentic sharing of your heart that you not only bring the process of manifesting your own value on the material plane, you are sharing with others the power of living from the heart.

Challenge: To share and use your resources for the greater good of the whole. To learn to manage resources judiciously so that they benefit the greatest number of people. To teach as a pathway of sharing.

Mastery: The ability to understand that knowledge and material resources are powerful, and to know how to use both as a path of service that sustains others and helps them grow their own abundant foundation.

Unbalanced: Diva energy. Selfish leadership that is rooted in lack and showing off. Holding back. Overcompensating for a lack of self-worth with narcissism. Fear of not being seen as a leader and reacting by being controlling or bombastic.

Writing Assignment:
Do you like to share? What do you have to give the world?

How do you own your right leadership? Are you comfortable as a leader? Do you shrink from leadership? Do you overcompensate by pushing too hard with your leadership?

Do you trust that when the right people are ready, you will be pressed into action as a leader and a teacher?

What do you need to heal, release, align, or bring to your awareness to trust your leadership energy more?

Affirmation:
I am a teacher and a leader. I use my resources, my knowledge, and my experience to expand the resources, knowledge, and experiences of others. I use my blessings of abundance to increase the blessings of others. I know that I am a vehicle of wisdom and knowledge. I sense when it's right for me to share who I am and what I know with others.

JUNE 13, 2021

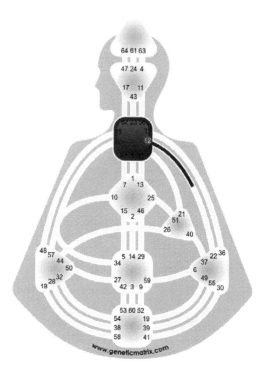

www.geneticmatrix.com

GATE 12: THE CHANNEL

 CHALLENGE:

To honor the self enough to wait for the right time and *mood* to speak. To know that *shyness* is actually a signal that the timing isn't right to share your transformational insights and expressions. When the timing IS right, to have the courage to share what you feel and sense. To honor the fact that your voice and the words you offer are a direct connection to Source and you channel the potential for transformation. To own your creative power.

JOURNAL QUESTIONS:

1. *How has shyness caused me to judge myself?*

2. *What do I need to do to cultivate a deeper connection with Source?*

3. *What do I need to do to connect more deeply with my creative power?*

 **AFFIRMATION:**

I am a creative being. My words, my self-expression, my creative offerings have the power to change the way people see and understand the world. I am a vessel of Divine Transformation and I serve Source through the words that I share. I wait for the right timing and when I am aligned with timing and flow, my creativity creates beauty and Grace in the world. I am a Divine Channel and I trust that the words that I serve will open the Hearts of others.

 EFT SETUP:

Even though I'm afraid that I'm failing my life purpose and mission, I now choose to know that I am in the right place fulfilling my right purpose. All I need to do is to follow my strategy, be deliberate, follow my heart, and all will be exactly as it needs to be, and I deeply and completely love and accept myself.

JUNE 19, 2021

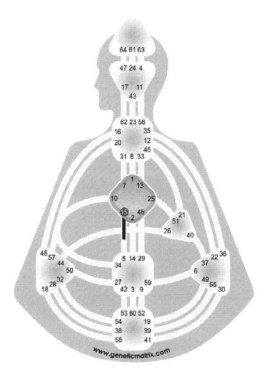

www.geneticmatrix.com

GATE 15: COMPASSION

 CHALLENGE:

To learn to allow yourself to be in the flow of your own rhythm. To not beat yourself up because you don't have daily *habits*. To have the courage to do the right thing even if you are worried about not having enough. To share from the Heart without giving up your Heart and serving as a *martyr*.

JOURNAL QUESTIONS:

1. Do I trust my own rhythm?

2. Do I share from the Heart? Do I over share? Does my sharing compromise my own Heart?

3. Do I judge my own rhythm? Can I find peace in aligning with my own rhythm?

4. What old patterns do I need to break?

 ## AFFIRMATION:

Like the power of a hurricane to transform the shoreline, my unique rhythm brings change to the landscape of my life and the world around me. I embrace my own rhythm and acknowledge the power of my own Heart. I share with ease and I serve my own Heart as the foundation of all I have to give the world.

 ## EFT SETUP:

Even though I feel powerless to make a difference in the world, I now choose to follow my heart and my passion knowing that I am the greatest gift I can give the world. The more I show up as my true self, the more I empower others to do the same and I deeply and completely love and accept myself.

June 24, 2021 - Full Moon

 Capricorn 3 degrees 28 minutes

 Gate 10 - The Gate of Self-Love

Full moon energy invites us to explore what we need to release and let go of in order to stay in alignment with our intentions.

Our New Moon in this cycle invites us to share the Heart of who we are. This Full Moon invites you to explore what might be keeping you from truly loving yourself. Self-love gives you the capacity to receive what you need to be able to give to the world. This moon invites us to explore whether we love ourselves enough to allow all the support and abundance that is waiting for us.

Self-love takes us out of victimhood perceptions and helps us reclaim our personal power and our personal sovereignty. This moon lovingly shines on us to help us release any old stories that have kept us disconnected from our lovability and our sense of empowerment over our life direction. Time to forgive yourself and others and to look at yourself through compassionate and loving eyes!

Challenge: To learn to love yourself. To learn to take responsibility for your own creations.

Mastery: To see your love for yourself as the source of your true creative power.

Unbalanced: To question your lovability or struggle to prove your love and worthiness. To give up and settle for less than what you deserve. To blame others for your circumstances and situations. To fall into victim consciousness.

Writing Assignment:

In what ways do you show love to yourself? Can you honestly say that you love yourself? What can you do to deepen your self-love?

Where can you find evidence of your lovability in your life right now?

What do you need to do to take responsibility for situations you hate in your life right now? What needs to change?

Where are you holding blame or victimhood in your life? How could you turn that energy around?

Affirmation:

I am an individuated aspect of the Divine. I am born of Love. My nature is to Love and be Loved. I am in the full flow of giving and receiving Love. I know that the quality of Love that I have for myself, sets the direction for what I attract into my life. I am constantly increasing the quality of love I experience and share with the world.

JUNE 25, 2021

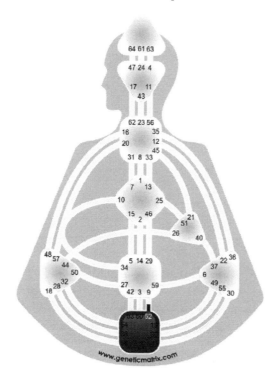

GATE 52: PERSPECTIVE

 **CHALLENGE:**

To learn to stay focused even when you're overwhelmed by a bigger perspective. To see the "big picture", to not let the massive nature of what you know confuse you and cause you to struggle with where to put your energy and attention.

 JOURNAL QUESTIONS:

1. *What do I do to maintain and sustain my focus? Is there anything in my environment or my life that I need to move out of the way in order for me to deepen my focus?*

2. *How do I manage feeling overwhelmed? What things am I avoiding because I feel overwhelmed by them? What is one bold action I can take to begin clearing the path for action?*

3. *How does my feeling of being overwhelmed affect my self-worth? How can I love myself more deeply in spite of feeling overwhelmed?*

 **AFFIRMATION:**

I am like the eagle soaring above the land. I see the entirety of what needs to happen to facilitate the evolution of the world. I use my perspective to see my unique and irreplaceable role in the Cosmic Plan. I see relationships and patterns that others don't always see. My perspective helps us all to build a peaceful world more effectively and in a consciously directed way.

 EFT SETUP:

Even though it makes me nervous to stop "doing" and sit with the stillness, I now trust the process and know that my state of alignment and clarity with my intentions is the most powerful thing I can do to create effectively and powerfully in my life. I relax, I trust and let my abundance unfold and I deeply and completely love and accept myself.

JULY 1, 2021

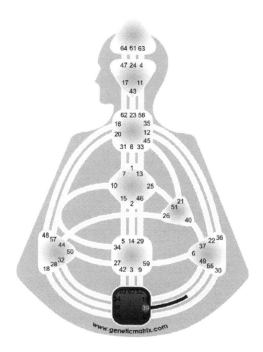

GATE 39: RECALIBRATION

 ## CHALLENGE:

To challenge and tease out energies that are not in alignment with faith and abundance. To bring them to awareness and to use them as pushing off points to deepen faith and trust in Source.

JOURNAL QUESTIONS:

1. *Do I trust Source? What do I need to do to deepen my trust in Source?*

2. *Do I feel like I am enough? Do I feel like I have enough?*

3. *Take stock of everything I have and everything I've been given. Do I have enough? Have I ever really not been supported?*

4. *What do I have that I'm grateful for?*

5. *Have I abdicated my own power to create? What needs to be healed, released, aligned or brought to my awareness to reactivate my power to create my own abundance?*

AFFIRMATION:

I am deeply calibrated with my faith. I trust that I am fully supported. I use experiences that create desire and wanting in me as opportunities to deepen my faith that I will receive and create all that I need to fulfill my mind, body and spirit. I am in the perfect flow of abundance and I am deeply aligned with Source.

 EFT SETUP:

Even though I worry about money, having the right relationship, and creating abundance in every area of my life, I now trust Spirit and allow the abundant nature of the Universe to reveal itself to me. I stay open to the possibilities of miracles and trust that all I have to do is stay conscious of the abundance of Spirit unfolding within me and I deeply and completely love and accept myself.

JULY 7, 2021

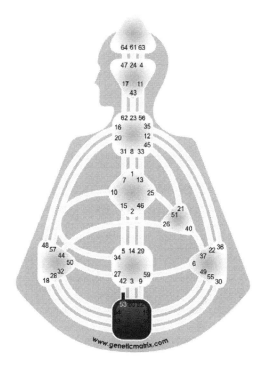

GATE 53: STARTING

 CHALLENGE:

To respond in alignment with your energy blueprint to opportunities to get things started. To initiate the process of preparing or "setting the state" for the manifestation of a dream before it becomes a reality. To learn to trust in the timing of the Universe and not take charge and try to implement your own ideas while working against Divine Timing. To not burn out trying to complete things. To find peace as a "starter," not a "finisher."

 JOURNAL QUESTIONS:

1. *How do I feel about myself when I have an idea and I can't get it initiated?*

2. *How do I feel when someone takes my initial idea and builds on it? Do I value what I started?*

3. *What identities and attachments do I have to being the one who starts and finishes something?*

4. *Do I judge myself for not finishing something? How can I be more gentle with myself?*

5. *Do I trust Divine Timing? How can I deepen my trust in right timing?*

 ## AFFIRMATION:

I am a servant to Divine Inspiration. My thoughts, inspirations and ideas set the stage for creative expansion and the potential for evolution. I take action on the ideas that present themselves to me in an aligned way. I honor all other ideas knowing that my gift is in the spark of energy that gets things rolling when the timing is right. While I wait for right timing, I guard my energy and charge my battery so that I am sustainable when the time is right for action.

 ## EFT SETUP:

Even though I'm scared to believe that my big dreams could come true, I now choose to trust the infinite power of the Universe and know that I am never given a dream that can't be fulfilled.

July 10, 2021 New Moon

 Cancer 18 degrees and 2 minutes

 Gate 53 - The Gate of Starting

New Moon energy invites us to explore how we can deepen our alignment with our intentions and asks us to focus on what we want to grow and expand on in our lives. The Gate 53 is one of the initiating Gates in Quantum Human Design. This New Moon, the energy of new beginnings, highlights the theme of new beginnings, so we experience a "double" new beginning this month.

The energy of the Gate 53 brings us the drive and motivation to get things started. We are inspired and eager to get going. The cautionary note here is to pay attention to the clues and cues that the Universe is sending you about which things to start. The energy here is about "getting started". To make the most of it, we must be starting the things that are correct and aligned for us. The things that are yours to start will reveal themselves this week.

New Moon energy is all about intention setting. We are praying for our next creative cycle to begin. Before you begin anything, make sure to take the time to send love and prayers to your creation. Anchor these and bring them into form with the correct energy. Take some time with this New Moon to really lovingly hold the intentions for your new idea! The next right step will reveal itself in due time!

Challenge: To respond (in alignment with your energy blueprint) to opportunities to get things started. To initiate the process of preparing or "setting the stage" for the manifestation of a dream before it becomes a reality. To learn to trust in the timing of the Universe and not take charge. To avoid trying to implement your own ideas while working against Divine Timing. To not burn out trying to complete things. To find peace as a "starter", not a "finisher".

Mastery: The ability to sit with inspiration and be attuned to what the Inspiration wants and needs. To launch the initiation sequence for an idea and then let the idea follow its right course with trust in the flow.

Unbalanced: Reacting to the pressure to get an idea started. To feel like a failure because everything you start against right timing fails. To be afraid to start anything because of the trauma of your past "failures". Starting everything and never reaping the rewards of what you start.

Writing Assignment:

How do you feel about yourself when you have an idea and you can't get it initiated?

How do you feel when someone takes your initial idea and builds on it? Do you value what you started?

What identities and attachments are connected to being the one who starts *and* finishes something?

Do you judge yourself for not finishing something? How can you be more gentle with yourself?

Do you trust Divine Timing? How can you deepen your trust in right timing?

Affirmation: I am a servant to Divine Inspiration. My thoughts, inspirations, and ideas set the stage for creative expansion and the potential for evolution. I take action on the ideas that present themselves to me in an aligned way. I honor all other ideas, knowing that my gift is in the spark of energy that gets things rolling when the timing is right. While I wait for right timing, I guard my energy and charge my battery so that I am sustainable when the time is right for action.

JULY 13, 2021

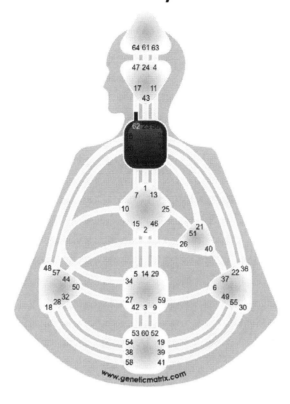

GATE 62: PREPARATION

CHALLENGE:

To trust that you'll be prepared for the next step. To not let worry and over-preparation detract you from being present in the moment. To let the fear of not being ready keep you trapped.

JOURNAL QUESTIONS:

1. *Do I worry? What do I do to manage my worry?*

2. *What can I do to trust that I know what I need to know? What proof do I have that I am in the flow of preparation?*

3. *Is there anything in my life right now that I need to plan for? Am I over-planning? Does my need for contingency plans keep me stuck?*

 **AFFIRMATION:**

I create the foundation for the practice of mastery by engineering the plan of action that creates growth. I am in the flow of my understanding and I use my knowledge and experience to be prepared for the evolution of what's next. I am ready and I am prepared. I trust my own preparation and allow myself to be in the flow of what's next knowing that I'll know what I need to know when I need to know it.

 EFT SETUP:

Even though I feel pressure to do something, I now choose to relax and trust the power of my dreams to call the right circumstance to me and I deeply and completely love and accept myself.

JULY 19, 2021

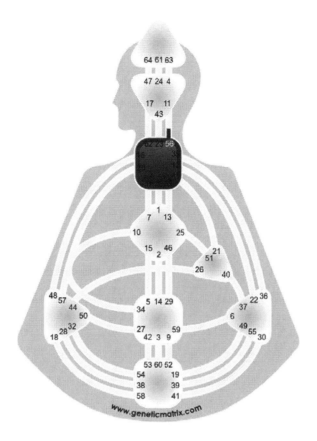

GATE 56: EXPANSION

 ## CHALLENGE:

To learn to share stories and inspirations with the right people at the right time. To learn to tell stories of expansion and not depletion and contraction.

 ## JOURNAL QUESTIONS:

1. *What stories do I share repeatedly with others? Do they lift people up or cause them to contract?*

2. *What stories do I tell about myself and my voice that cause me to either expand or contract?*

3. *What am I here to inspire others to do or be?*

 ## AFFIRMATION:

I am a Divine Storyteller. The stories of possibility that I share have the power to inspire others to grow and expand. I use my words as a template for possibility and expansion for the world. I inspire the world with my words.

 ## EFT SETUP:

Even though I'm afraid to share my ideas, I now choose to take leadership with my inspirations and share my precious ideas with others and I deeply and completely love and accept myself.

July 24, 2021 - Full Moon

 Aquarius 1 degree and 26 minutes

 Gate 60 - The Gate of Conservation

Full moon energy invites us to explore what we need to release and let go of in order to stay in alignment with our intentions.

The Gate 60 is an important energy that supports innovation. We entered into this moon cycle with the energy for starting. Now we are looking at what we need to "bring" with us as we innovate and move forward.

The Gate 60 encourages us to explore what IS working in our lives? Starting new doesn't always mean that we have to burn everything down and start over. Innovation builds upon what has come before. The Gate 60 encourages us to be grateful for the things that we have and encourages us to build on what we know works. Gratitude is simply focus with Heart. What are you grateful for this week? What perspectives do you need to release in order to be better able to see what you have?

Challenge: To not let the fear of loss overwhelm your resourcefulness. To learn to find what is working and focus on it instead of looking at the loss and disruption.

Mastery: The ability to find the blessings in transformation. Optimism. To know how to focus on what is working instead of what's not.

Unbalanced: To hold on and not allow for growth. To fight for the old and rebuke change. To let the overwhelm of change and disruption create paralysis and resistance.

Writing Assignment:

What change are you resisting? What are you afraid of?

What are the things in your life that are working that you need to focus on?

Is your fear of loss holding you back?

Affirmation: I am grateful for all the transformation and change in my life. I know that disruption is the catalyst for my growth. I am able to find the blessings of the past and incorporate them in my innovative vision for the future. I am optimistic about the future and I transform the world by growing what works.

JULY 25, 2021

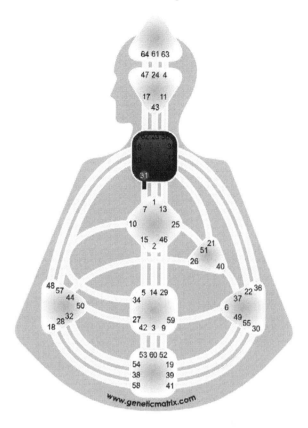

GATE 31: THE LEADER

 ## CHALLENGE:

To learn to lead as a representative of the people you are leading. To cultivate a leadership agenda of service. To not let your fear of not being seen, heard or accepted get in the way of healthy leadership. To learn to take your rightful place as a leader and not hide out.

JOURNAL QUESTIONS:

1. *How do I feel about being a leader? Am I comfortable leading? Do I shrink from taking leadership?*

2. *What is my place of service? Who do I serve?*

 **AFFIRMATION:**

I am a natural born leader. I serve at my highest potential when I am empowering others by giving them a voice and then serving their needs. I use my power to lead people to a greater expansion of who they are and to support them in increasing their abundance, sustainability and peace.

 EFT SETUP:

Even though I'm afraid to be seen, I now choose to express myself and the magnificence that is me with gusto, courage, awareness of my own power and preciousness and I deeply and completely love and accept myself.

JULY 30, 2021

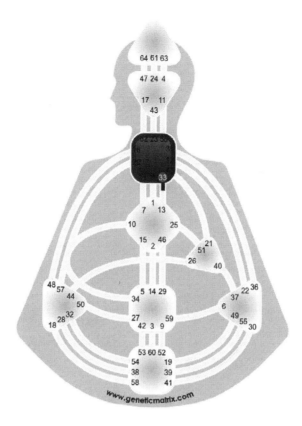

GATE 33: RETELLING

 ## CHALLENGE:

To learn to share a personal narrative that reflects your true value and your worth. To share a personal narrative when it serves the intention to serve, improving the direction of others. To share history in an empowering way.

 ## JOURNAL QUESTIONS:

1. *What personal narratives am I telling that might be keeping me stuck, feeling like a victim, or feeling unlovable? How can I rewrite these stories?*

2. *What listening practices do I have? What can I do to listen better so that I can gauge when it is the right time to share in a powerful way?*

 **AFFIRMATION:**

I am a processor of stories. My gift is my ability to help others find the blessings, the love and the power from stories of pain. I hold people's secrets and stories and transform them to share when the time is right. The stories I tell change the direction of people's lives. I use the power of stories to increase the power of Heart in the world and to help build a world of Love.

 EFT SETUP:

Even though my stories from my past have held me back, I now choose to rewrite the story of my life and tell it the way I choose, with forgiveness, embracing the gifts and honoring my courage and strength in my story and I deeply and completely love and accept myself.

AUGUST 5, 2021

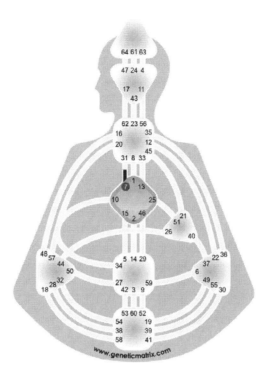

www.geneticmatrix.com

GATE 7: COLLABORATION

 ## CHALLENGE:

To master the need to be in front and allow yourself to serve through building teams, collaborating and influencing the figurehead of leadership. To be at peace with serving the leader through support and collaboration. To recognize that the voice of the leader is only as strong and powerful as the support he/she receives.

JOURNAL QUESTIONS:

1. *What are my gifts and strengths? How do I use those gifts to influence and lead others?*

2. *How do I feel about not being the figurehead of leadership? What happens when I only support the leadership? Do I still feel powerful? Influential?*

3. *Make a list of the times when my influence has positively directed leadership.*

 **AFFIRMATION:**

I am an agent of peace who influences the direction and organization of leadership. I unify people around ideas. I influence with my wisdom, my knowledge and my connections. I am a team builder, a collaborator, and I organize people in ways that empower them and support them in creating a collective direction rooted in compassion.

 EFT SETUP:

Even though I feel confused and conflicted about what to do, I trust the Divine Flow and let the Universe show me the right thing to do in the right time and I deeply and completely love, trust and accept myself.

August 8, 2021 - New Moon

 Leo 16 degrees and 14 minutes

 Gate 7 - The Gate of Collaboration

New Moon energy invites us to explore how we can deepen our alignment with our intentions and asks us to focus on what we want to grow and expand on in our lives. The Gate 7 often gives us a challenge. This energy instills in us a longing for leadership, but this isn't the leadership energy of ego. This is the power to work with others and collaborate on changing our direction and future together. We have to learn to surrender our egos and embrace our place of serving the greater good with this week.

This new moon invites us to begin new collaborations, and to build teams of people unified around new ideas willing to explore new directions. This is a powerful intention-setting time that encourages us to explore how we can better work together or support others who are fulfilling the leadership that takes us where we want to go.

Challenge: To master the need to be in front and allow yourself to serve through building teams, collaborating, and influencing the figurehead of leadership. To be at peace with serving the leader through support and collaboration. To recognize that the voice of the leader is only as strong and powerful as the support he/she receives.

Mastery: To embrace that power comes from supporting, influencing and collaborating with leadership. To recognize that you don't have to be the figurehead to influence the direction that leadership assumes. The chief of staff is often more powerful than the president. The energy to unify people around an idea that influences the direction of leadership.

Unbalanced: To struggle and fight to be seen and recognized as *the* leader at cost to your energy and the fulfillment of your purpose.

Writing Assignment:

What are your gifts and strengths? How do you use those gifts to influence and lead others?

How do you feel about not being the figurehead of leadership? What happens when you "only" support the leadership? Do you still feel powerful? Influential?

Make a list of the times when your influence has positively directed leadership?

Affirmation: I am an agent of peace who influences the direction and organization of leadership. I unify people around ideas. I influence with my wisdom, my knowledge, and my connections. I am a team builder, a collaborator, and I organize people in ways that empower and support them in creating a collective direction rooted in compassion.

AUGUST 11, 2021

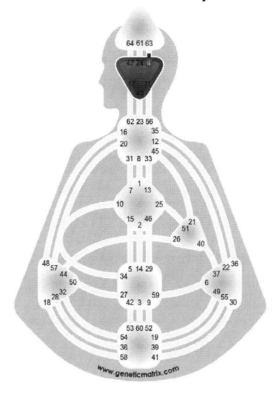

GATE 4: POSSIBILITY

 ## CHALLENGE:

To learn to embrace ideas as possibilities, not answers, and to let the power of the possibility stimulate the imagination as a way of calibrating the emotions and the Heart. This Gate teaches us the power of learning to wait to see which possibility actually manifests in the physical world and to experiment with options in response.

 ## JOURNAL QUESTIONS:

1. *What ideas do I have right now that need me to nurture and activate them?*

2. *What possibilities do these ideas stimulate right now? Take some time to write or visualize the possibilities.*

3. *Am I comfortable with waiting? What can I do to increase my patience and curiosity?*

AFFIRMATION:

I am tuned into the cosmic flow of possibility. I am inspired about exploring new possibilities and potentials. I use the power of my thoughts to stretch the limits of what is known and engage my imagination to explore the potential of the unknown.

EFT SETUP:

Even though I don't know what to do, I allow my questions to seed the Universe and I trust and wait with great patience that the answers will be revealed to me and I deeply and completely love and accept myself.

AUGUST 17, 2021

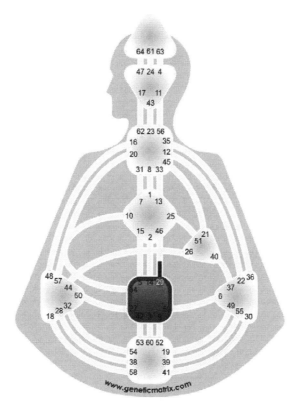

www.geneticmatrix.com

GATE 29: DEVOTION

 ## CHALLENGE:

To discover what and who you need to devote yourself to. To sustain yourself so that you can sustain your devotion. To learn to say "no" to what you need to say "no" to and to learn to "yes" to what you want to say "yes" to.

 ## JOURNAL QUESTIONS:

1. *What devotion do I have right now that drives me? Is this a devotion that inspires me or do I feel overly obligated to it?*

2. *Who would I be and what would I choose if I gave myself permission to say "no" more often?*

3. *What would I like to say "no" to that I am saying "yes" to right now?*

4. *What obligations do I need to take off my plate right now?*

5. *What would I like to devote myself to?*

 ## AFFIRMATION:

I have an extraordinary ability to devote myself to the manifestation of an idea. My commitment to my story and to the fulfillment of my intention changes the story of what's possible in my own life and for humanity. I choose my commitments with great care. I devote myself to what's vital for the evolution of the world and I nurture myself first because my well-being is the foundation of what I create.

 ## EFT SETUP:

Even though I'm afraid to invest all my effort into my dream...what if it fails...what if I'm crazy...what if I just need to buckle down and be "normal"...I now choose to do it anyway and I deeply and completely love and accept myself.

August 22, 2021 - Full Moon

 Aquarius 29 degrees and 37 minutes

 Gate 30 - The Gate of Passion

Full moon energy invites us to explore what we need to release and let go of in order to stay in alignment with our intentions.

The Gate 30 is an energy that carries a lot of intensity. It gives the energy that fuels an idea or an inspiration, giving you the passion to do the work necessary to nurture an idea into form, even when the work is hard or if you can't see evidence of it coming true yet.

People who carry this energy have a tendency to be intense. Burnout is a shadow aspect of this intense energy.

This Full Moon encourages us to explore what brings us passion, or to discover where we need to reconnect with that passion, and also what we need to do to increase the energy around our dreams and ideas. It's also inviting us to explore whether we need rest or restoration in order to sustain our passion, and to ensure that we stay strong and resilient on our creative path.

Challenge: To be able to sustain a dream or a vision without burning out. To know which dream to be passionate about. To not let passion overwhelm you and to wait for the right timing to share your passion with the world.

Mastery: The ability to sustain a dream, intention, and a vision until you bring it into form. To inspire others with the power of your dream. To inspire passion in others.

Unbalanced: Burnout. Impatience and not waiting for the right timing. Misdirected passion that is perceived as too much intensity. Leaping into chaos.

Writing Assignment:

What are you passionate about? Have you lost your passion?

How is your energy? Are you physically burned out? Are you burned out on your ideas?

What do you need to do to sustain your vision or dream about what you are inspired to create in your life?

Do you have a dream or vision you are avoiding because you're afraid it won't come true?

Affirmation: I am a passionate creator. I use the intensity of my passion to increase my emotional energy and sustain the power of my dream and what I imagine for Life. I trust in the Divine flow and I wait for the right timing and the right circumstances to act on my dream.

AUGUST 23, 2021

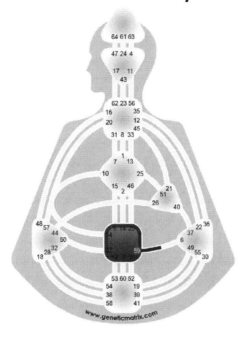

GATE 59: SUSTAINABILITY

 ## CHALLENGE:

To learn to make abundant choices that sustain you, and at the same time, others. To collaborate and initiate others into sustainable relationships from a place of sufficiency. To learn to share what you have in a sustainable way.

 ## JOURNAL QUESTIONS:

1. *Do I trust in my own abundance?*

2. *How do I feel about sharing what I have with others?*

3. *Am I creating relationship and partnership agreements that honor my work?*

4. *Do I have relationships and agreements that are draining me? What needs to change?*

5. *How do I feel about being "right"? Am I open to other ways of thinking or being? Do I believe in creating agreements and alignments with people who have different values and perspectives?*

 **AFFIRMATION:**

The energy that I carry has the power to create sufficiency and sustainability for all. I craft valuable alliances and agreements that support me in expanding abundance for everyone. I hold to higher principles and values that are rooted in my trust in sufficiency and the all-providing Source. Through my work and alignments my blessings serve to increase the blessings of myself and others.

 EFT SETUP:

Even though I struggle to share my intentions, I now choose to boldly state my intentions and wait for the pieces of my creation to magically fall into place and I deeply and completely love and accept myself.

AUGUST 29, 2021

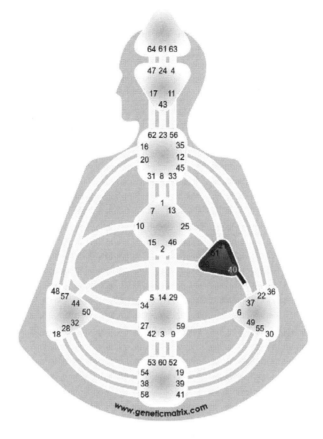

GATE 40: RESTORATION

 ## CHALLENGE:

To learn to value yourself enough to retreat from community and the energy of those you love to restore, restock and replenish your inner resources. To learn to interpret the signal of loneliness correctly. To take responsibility for your own care and resources and to not abdicate your own power to take care of yourself.

 ## JOURNAL QUESTIONS:

1. *What role does loneliness play in my life? Has loneliness caused me to doubt my value?*

2. *What do I need to do to restore my energy? Am I doing enough to take care of myself?*

3. *What agreements am I making in my relationships that might be causing me to compromise my value? How can I rewrite these agreements?*

4. *Am I abdicating my responsibility for my self-care? Am I living a "martyr" model? What needs to be healed, released, aligned and brought to my awareness for me to take responsibility for cultivating my own sense of value and my self-worth?*

 ## AFFIRMATION:

I am a powerful resource for my community. The energy that I hold impacts others deeply and brings them to deeper states of alignment and sustainability. I take care of my body, mind and soul because I know that the more that I am and the more that I have, the more I can give to others. I take care of myself first because I know that good things flow from me. I am valuable and powerful and I claim and defend the true story of Who I Truly Am.

 ## EFT SETUP:

Even though it is hard to let go of the obligations of relationships, I now choose to release all relationships that are draining and unsupportive and I deeply and completely love and accept myself.

SEPTEMBER 3, 2021

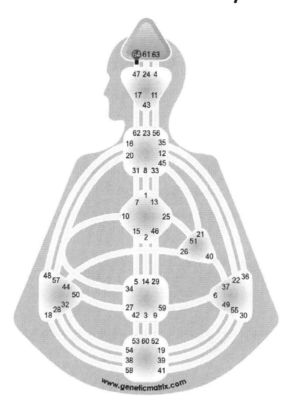

GATE 64: DIVINE TRANSFERENCE

 ## CHALLENGE:

To not let the power of your big ideas overwhelm you and shut down your dreaming and creating. To not get lost in the pressure of answering the question "how."

 ## JOURNAL QUESTIONS:

1. *What do I do to take care of my Big Ideas?*

2. *How do I feel about having "dreams" but not always the solutions?*

3. *How can I stop judging the gift of my dreams?*

4. *Do I trust that the "how" of my ideas will be revealed? How can I deepen this trust?*

 **AFFIRMATION:**

I am a conduit for expansive thinking. My inspirations and ideas create the seeds of possibility in my mind and in the mind of others. I honor the dreams that pass through my mind and allow my big ideas to stimulate my imagination and the imagination of others. I trust the Universe to reveal the details of my dreams when the time is right. I use the power of my dreams to stimulate a world of possibility and expansion.

 EFT SETUP:

Even though I don't know what's next, I wait and trust that the perfect right step will show up for me and I deeply and completely love and accept myself.

Even though I feel overwhelmed with ideas, I trust the Universe to reveal the next step to me. I relax and wait and I deeply and completely love and accept myself.

September 7, 2021 New Moon

 Virgo 14 degrees 38 minutes

 Gate 64 - The Gate of Divine Transference

New Moon energy invites us to explore how we can deepen our alignment with our intentions and asks us to focus on what we want to grow and expand on in our lives. The Gate 64 brings us (very) big ideas! This energy often gives us ideas that seem so big, it can feel overwhelming. This is inspiration in its purest form. We are inspired by an idea that if not accompanied with instructions, leaves us spinning with the awe of the concept but feeling confused about how to begin to make the concept a reality.

The trick to working with the Gate 64 is to remember that the inspiration is usually followed by an epiphany! We are given the next right step when we wait patiently and enjoy the inspiration in the meantime. This New Moon is inviting us to dream, to imagine, to not let confusion overwhelm us, but to let the ideas percolate until the timing is right for us to be given the next right step to making our dream come true.

Challenge: To not let the power of your big ideas overwhelm you and shut down your dreaming and creating. To get lost in the pressure of answering the question "how"?

Mastery: The ability to receive a "big idea" and to serve the idea by giving it your imagination and dreaming. To trust that you'll know how to implement the idea if it is yours to make manifest. To hold the energy of an idea for the world.

Unbalanced: To feel pressure to try to "manifest" a big idea. To feel despairing or inadequate or ungrounded if you don't know how to make an idea a reality. To feel deep mental pressure to "figure" out an idea. To give up dreaming.

Writing Assignment:

What do you do to take care of your Big Ideas?

How do you feel about having "dreams" but not always the solutions?

How can you stop judging the gift of your dreams?

Do you trust that the "how" of your ideas will be revealed? How can you deepen this trust?

Affirmation: I am a conduit for expansive thinking. My inspirations and ideas create the seeds of possibility in my mind and in the minds of others. I honor the dreams that pass through my mind and allow my big ideas to stimulate my imagination and the imagination of others. I trust the Universe to reveal the details of my dreams when the time is right. I use the power of my dreams to stimulate a world of possibility and expansion.

SEPTEMBER 9, 2021

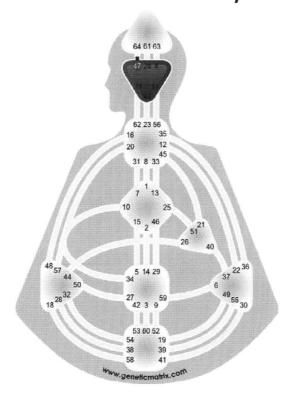

GATE 47: MINDSET

 ### CHALLENGE:

To master a mindset of open-ness and possibility. To not let inspiration die because you don't know "how" to fulfill it.

 ### JOURNAL QUESTIONS:

1. *What thoughts do I have when I receive an idea or inspiration? Am I hopeful or despairing? How does it feel to let go of figuring out "how" I'm going to make my idea a reality?*

2. *What do I do to regulate my mindset? What practices do I need to cultivate to increase the power of my thoughts?*

 **AFFIRMATION:**

My mindset is the source of my inspired actions and attitude. I know that when I receive an idea and inspiration it is my job to nurture the idea by using the power of my imagination to increase the potential and emotional frequency of the idea. I consistently keep my inner and outer environment aligned with the energy of possibility and potential. I know that it is my job to create by virtue of my alignment and I relax knowing that it's the job of the Universe to fulfill my inspirations.

 EFT SETUP:

Even though it's frustrating to not know how to make something happen, I now choose to wait for Divine Insight and I trust that the right information will be revealed to me at the perfect time and I deeply and completely love and accept myself.

SEPTEMBER 15, 2021

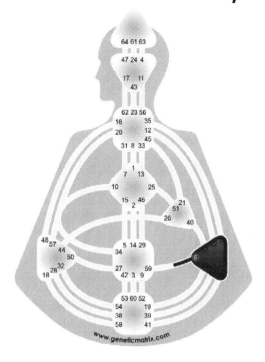

GATE 6: IMPACT

 ## CHALLENGE:

The ability to master emotional energy and learn to trust that your impact is in service to the world. When you understand that your life is a vehicle for service and your energy is being used to influence and impact those around you, you assume greater obligation and responsibility to maintaining a high frequency of energy. The quality of the emotional energy you cultivate influences others to come together in an equitable, sustainable and peaceful way. Learning to trust that your words and impact will have effect when the timing is correct and not overriding Divine Timing.

JOURNAL QUESTIONS:

1. *What do I need to do to deepen my trust in Divine Timing?*

2. *What do I need to do to prepare myself to be seen and to have influence?*

3. *What do I need to do to sustain my emotional energy in order to align with peaceful and sustainable solutions?*

4. *How do I feel about lack? How do I feel about abundance? How can I create a greater degree of emotional abundance in my life? In my daily practice?*

 ## AFFIRMATION:

My emotional energy influences the world around me. I am rooted in the energy of equity, sustainability and peace. When I am aligned with abundance, I am an energetic source of influence that facilitates elegant solutions to creating peace and well-being. I am deliberate and aligned with values that create peace in my life, in my community and in the world.

 ## EFT SETUP:

Even though I'm ready to leap into action, I now choose to take a breath, wait out my emotions and trust that the right timing will be revealed to me. I'm not missing out on anything. Divine Order is the rule of the day and I deeply and completely love and accept myself.

September 20, 2021 - Full Moon

 Pisces 28 degrees 14 minutes

 Gate 36 - The Gate of Exploration

Full moon energy invites us to explore what we need to release and let go of in order to stay in alignment with our intentions.

The Gate 36 is a powerful Gate that often brings us experiences that can help us break free from old patterns. The Gate 36 brings us the exploration of what else is possible. It invites us to shatter our attachment to old patterns of behavior and to let go of our need to "reason" our way through a challenge.

The Full Moon invites us to explore where we may have limited ourselves because of old expectations. The Moon wants us to take a leap, to try something new, to stay in a state of expectation that the solution to the challenges we face can be re-solved in new ways. The energy brings us the potential for miraculous outcomes if we let go of the idea that the answer has to fit into our previous paradigm. It's time to allow for something completely different!

Challenge: To not let boredom cause you to leap into chaos. To learn to stick with something long enough to become masterful and to bear the fruits of your experience.

Mastery: The ability to hold a vision and sustain it with an aligned frequency of emotional energy and to bring the vision into form when the timing is right. The ability to stretch the boundaries of the story of Humanity by breaking patterns. Creating miracles through emotional alignment.

Unbalanced: Not waiting for the right timing and leaping into new opportunities without waiting for alignment, causing chaos. To leap from opportunity to opportunity without waiting to see how the story will play out and never getting to experience the full fruition of the experience.

Writing Assignment:

How does boredom impact your life? What do you do when you feel bored? What can you do to keep yourself aligned even when you're bored?

What stories have you experienced that have shattered old patterns and expectations? How have your stories changed or inspired others?

What do you do to maintain or sustain emotional alignment? What do you need to add to your daily practice to "amp" up your emotional energy around your intentions?

Affirmation: My experiences and stories break old patterns and push the boundaries of the edge of what's possible for humanity. I defy the patterns and I create miracles through my emotional alignment with possibility. I hold my vision and maintain my emotional energy as I wait to bear the fruit of my intentions and my visions.

SEPTEMBER 21, 2021

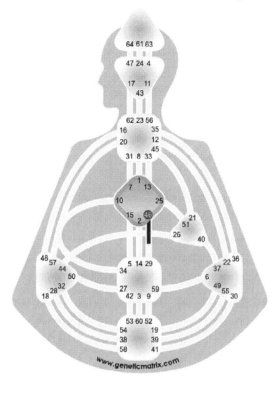

www.geneticmatrix.com

GATE 46: EMBODIMENT

 ## CHALLENGE:

To learn to love your body. To learn to fully be in your body. To learn to love the sensual nature of your physical form and to move it with love and awareness.

 ## JOURNAL QUESTIONS:

1. *Do I love my body? What can I do to deepen my love for my body?*

2. *What parts of my body do I love and appreciate? Make a list of every part of my body that I love.*

3. *What do I need to do to amplify the life force I am experiencing in my body?*

4. *What kinds of devotion and commitment do I experience that help me harness greater amounts of life force in my body? How can I deepen my commitment and devotion to my body?*

 ## AFFIRMATION:

My body is the vehicle for my soul. My ability to fully express who I am and my life and soul purpose is deeply rooted in my body's ability to carry my soul. I love, nurture and commit to my body. I appreciate all of its miraculous abilities and form. Every day I love my body more.

 ## EFT SETUP:

Even though it's hard for me to love my body, I now choose to embrace my amazing physical form and honor it for all the good it brings me, and I deeply and completely love and accept myself.

SEPTEMBER 27, 2021

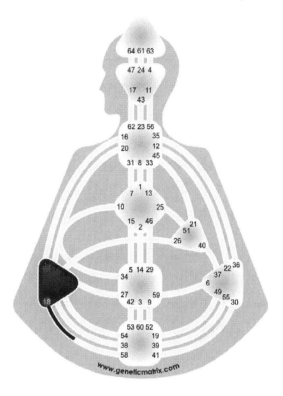

www.geneticmatrix.com

GATE 18: RE-ALIGNMENT

 ## CHALLENGE:

To learn to wait for the right timing and the right circumstances to offer your intuitive insights into how to fix or correct a pattern. To wait for the right time and the right reason to share your critique. To understand that the purpose of re-alignment is to create more joy, not to be "right".

 ## JOURNAL QUESTIONS:

1. *What does joy mean to me? How do I serve it?*

2. *How do I cultivate joy in my own life?*

3. *How does it feel to be "right" about something and keep it to myself? Do I need to release any old "stories" about needing to be "right"?*

4. *Do I trust my own insights? Do I have the courage to share them when it's necessary?*

 **AFFIRMATION:**

I am a powerful force that re-aligns patterns. My insights and awareness gives people the information they need to deepen their mastery and to experience greater joy. I serve joy and I align the patterns of the world to increase the world's potential for living in the flow of joy.

 EFT SETUP:

Even though I feel criticized and judged, I now choose to hear the wisdom of the correction and release my personal attachment and I deeply and completely love and accept myself.

OCTOBER 2, 2021

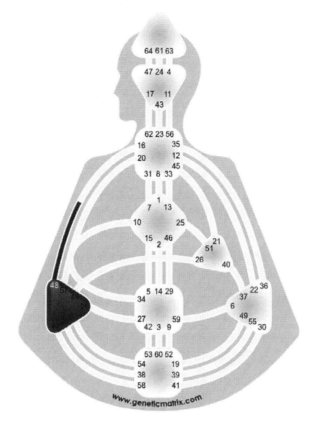

GATE 48: WISDOM

CHALLENGE:

To allow yourself to trust that you'll know what you need to know when you need to know it. To not let the fear of not knowing stop you from creating. To not let "not knowing" hold you back.

JOURNAL QUESTIONS:

1. *Do I trust my own knowing? What needs to be healed, released, aligned and brought to my awareness for me to deepen my self-trust?*

2. *What practice do I have that keeps me connected to the wisdom of Source? How can I deepen my connection to Source?*

 **AFFIRMATION:**

I am a depth of wisdom and knowledge. My studies and experiences have taught me everything I need to know. I push beyond the limits of my earthly knowledge and take great leaps of faith as a function of my deep connection to Source knowing that I'll always know what I need to know when I need to know it.

 EFT SETUP:

Even though I'm afraid I'm not ready to, I now choose to courageously dive in and just do it and I deeply and completely love and accept myself.

October 6, 2021 - New Moon

 Libra 13 degrees and 25 minutes

 Gate 48 - The Gate of Wisdom

New Moon energy invites us to explore how we can deepen our alignment with our intentions and asks us to focus on what we want to grow and expand on in our lives. The Gate 48 gives us the energy for diving deep into information, practice, and experience. This is an energy that often prevents us from starting something new because the Gate 48 demands that we have a depth of knowledge and experience in place in order for us to feel comfortable enough to take a leap and try something new. We often experience this energy as a fear of inadequacy.

With the New Moon highlighting this theme, the light of the Moon is encouraging us to trust that we know enough, and that we'll know what we need to know when we need to know it. We are learning that if we have faith in our own wisdom and have the courage to take a leap forward - even though we may be way out of our comfort zone - we'll know what we need to know when we need to know it and we'll discover that we're far more prepared than we realized.

Challenge: To allow yourself to trust that you'll know what you need to know when you need to know it. To not let the fear of not knowing stop you from creating. To not let "not knowing" hold you back.

Mastery: The wisdom to explore and learn the depth of knowledge necessary to create a strong foundation for action and mastery. The self-trust to have faith in your ability to know how to know, and to trust your connection to Source as the true source of your knowledge.

Unbalanced: Paralysis in inadequacy. To be afraid to try something new or to go beyond your comfort zone because you think you don't know or that you're not ready.

Writing Assignment:
Do you trust your own knowing? What needs to be healed, released, aligned and brought to your awareness for you to deepen your self- trust?
What practice do you have that keeps you connected to the wisdom of Source? How can you deepen your connection to Source?

Affirmation: I am a depth of wisdom and knowledge. My studies and experiences have taught me everything I need to know. I push beyond the limits of my earthly knowledge and take great leaps of faith as a function of my deep connection to Source, knowing that I'll always know what I need to know when I need to know it.

OCTOBER 8, 2021

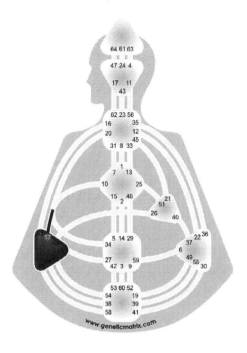

GATE 57: INSTINCT

CHALLENGE:

To learn to trust your own insights and "gut". To learn to tell the difference between an instinctive response versus a fear of the future. To master your connection to your sense of "right" timing.

JOURNAL QUESTIONS:

1. *Do I trust my intuition? What does my intuition feel like to me?*

2. *Sometimes doing a retrospective analysis of my intuition/instinct makes it more clear how my intuitive signal works. What experiences in the past have I had that I "knew" I should or shouldn't do? How have I experienced my intuition in the past?*

3. *When I think about moving forward in my life, do I feel afraid? What am I afraid of? What can I do to mitigate the fear?*

4. *What impulses am I experiencing that are telling me to prepare for what's next in my life? Am I acting on my impulses? Why or why not?*

AFFIRMATION:

My Inner Wisdom is deeply connected to the pulse of Divine Timing. I listen to my Inner Wisdom and follow my instinct. I know when and how to prepare the way to prepare for the future. I take guided action and I trust myself and Source.

 ## EFT SETUP:

Even though it's scary to trust my gut, I now choose to honor my awareness, quiet my mind and go with what feels right and I deeply and completely love and accept myself.

OCTOBER 14, 2021

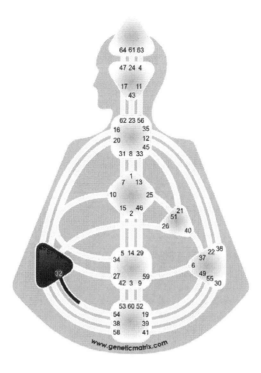

GATE 32: ENDURANCE

 ## CHALLENGE:

To trust in Divine Timing. To prepare for the next step of manifestation and to align with the unfolding of the process. To be patient.

 ## JOURNAL QUESTIONS:

1. *What do I need to do to be prepared to manifest my vision? What actionable steps need to be completed in order for me to be ready when the timing is right?*

2. *What do I need to do to cultivate patience?*

3. *Do I have a fear of failing that is causing me to avoid being prepared?*

4. *Am I over-doing and being overly prepared? Am I pushing too hard? What can I let go of?*

 ## AFFIRMATION:

I am a divine translator for Divine Inspiration. I sense and know what needs to be prepared on the earthly plane in order to be ready for right timing. I am aligned with right timing and I prepare and wait patiently knowing that when the time is right, I am ready to do the work to help transform pain into power.

 ## EFT SETUP:

Even though I've worked hard to make my dreams come true and nothing has happened yet, I trust in Divine Timing and keep tending to my vision and I deeply and completely love and accept myself.

OCTOBER 19, 2021

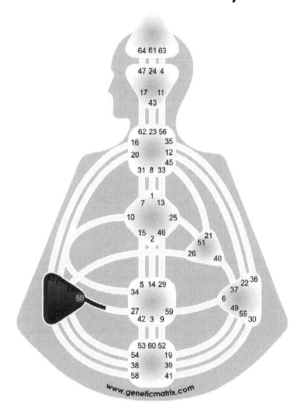

GATE 50: NURTURING

CHALLENGE:

To transcend guilt and unhealthy obligation and do what you need to do to take care of yourself in order to better serve others. To hold to rigid principles to judge others.

JOURNAL QUESTIONS:

1. *How do I feel about taking care of myself first? How do I sustain my nurturing energy?*

2. *What role does guilt play in driving and/or motivating me? What would I choose if I could remove the guilt?*

3. *Do I have non-negotiable values? What are they? How do I handle people who share different values from me?*

 **AFFIRMATION:**

My presence brings Love into the room. I nurture and love others. I take care of myself first in order to be better able to serve Love. I intuitively know what people need and I facilitate for them a state of self-love and self-empowerment by helping them align more deeply with the power of Love. I let go and I allow others to learn from what I model and teach. I am a deep well of love that sustains the planet.

 EFT SETUP:

Even though it's hard for me to give and receive love, I now choose to be completely open to receiving and sharing deep and unconditional love starting by deeply and completely loving and accepting myself first.

October 20, 2021 - Full Moon

 Aries 27 degrees and 26 minutes

 Gate 3 - The Gate of innovation

Full moon energy invites us to explore what we need to release and let go of in order to stay in alignment with our intentions.

The Gate 3 brings us the energy of change and transformation. This is important energy that has the potential to change the way in which we work and the kind of work we do in the world. This energy invites us to engage in exploring new ways to do things.

The innovation of the Gate 3 is often blocked by our unwillingness to explore the past and what has come before. Sometimes when we innovate, we want to move forward with such speed and intention that we can tend to "throw the baby out with the bath water". This Full Moon encourages us to look at what has come before and find the threads of what DID work, what IS going well, and what we want to bring forward with us as we transform and evolve.

Gratitude is an essential component to innovation. We can't move forward until we either release the lessons of the past or we bring the things that served us well with us. Gratitude forces us to explore the gifts from the past that we need to build upon to innovate.

Challenge: To learn to trust in Divine Timing and to know that your ideas and insights will be transmitted to the world when the world is ready.

Mastery: The ability to embrace and integrate new ideas and new ways of doing things. To learn to stay in appreciation for your unique way of thinking and being and to trust that, as an innovator on the leading edge of consciousness, your time to transmit what you're here to bring forth will come, so you wait and cultivate your ideas with patience.

Unbalanced: To feel pressured and panicked about the need to share an idea or innovation. To burn yourself out trying to override Divine Timing.

Writing Assignment:

Where has Divine Timing worked out in your life? What has waiting taught you?

Do you trust in Divine Timing?

If the opportunity to share your ideas with the world presented itself today, would you be ready? If not, what do you need to prepare to be ready?

Affirmation: I am here to bring change to the world. My natural ability to see what else is possible and to create something new are my strengths and my gifts. I patiently cultivate my inspiration and use my understanding of what is needed to help evolve the world.

OCTOBER 25, 2021

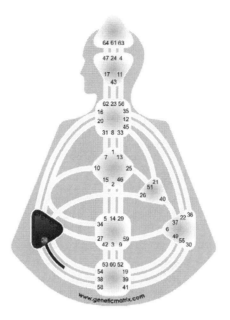

GATE 28: ADVENTURE/CHALLENGE

 ## CHALLENGE:

To not let struggle and challenge leave you feeling defeated and despairing. To learn to face life as an adventure. Do not let challenge and struggle cause you to feel as if you've failed.

 ## JOURNAL QUESTIONS:

1. *How can I turn my challenge into adventure?*

2. *Where do I need to cultivate a sense of adventure in my life?*

3. *What do I need to do to rewrite the story of my "failures"?*

4. *What meanings, blessings and lessons have I learned from my challenges?*

5. *What needs to be healed, released, aligned and brought to my awareness for me to trust myself and my choices?*

6. *What do I need to do to forgive myself for my perceived past failures?*

 **AFFIRMATION:**

I am here to push the boundaries of life and what is possible. I thrive in situations that challenge me. I am an explorer on the leading edge of consciousness and my job is to test how far I can go. I embrace challenge. I am an adventurer. I share all that I have learned from my challenges with the world. My stories help give people greater meaning, teach them what is truly worthy of creating and inspire people to transform.

 EFT SETUP:

Even though everything feels hard, I now trust that I am mastering what is truly important in my life. I trust the lessons the Universe brings me and I deeply and completely love and accept myself.

OCTOBER 31, 2021

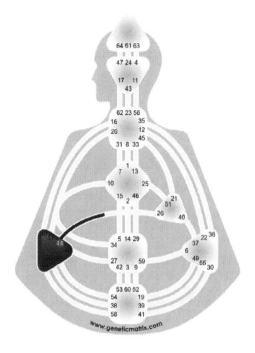

GATE 44: TRUTH

CHALLENGE:

To not get stuck in past patterns. To cultivate the courage to go forward without being stuck in the fear of the past. To learn how to transform pain into power and to have the courage to express your authentic self without compromising or settling.

JOURNAL QUESTIONS:

1. *What patterns from the past are holding me back from moving forward with courage?*

2. *Do I see how my experiences from the past have helped me learn more about Who I Truly Am? What have I learned about my value and my power?*

3. *What needs to be healed, released, aligned and brought to my awareness for me to fully activate my power?*

4. *What needs to be healed, released, aligned and brought to my awareness for me to step boldly into my aligned and authentic path?*

 **AFFIRMATION:**

I am powerfully intuitive and can sense the patterns that keep others stuck in limiting beliefs and constricted action. Through my insights and awareness I help others break free from past limiting patterns and learn to find the power in their pain, find the blessings in their challenges and help them align more deeply with an authentic awareness of their True Value and Purpose.

 EFT SETUP:

Even though it's hard for me to let go, I deeply and completely love and accept myself.

Even though I am afraid to repeat the past, I now move forward with confidence trusting that I have learned what I needed to learn. I can create whatever future I desire, and I deeply and completely love and accept myself.

November 4, 2021 - New Moon

 Scorpio 12 degrees and 40 minutes

 Gate 44 - The Gate of Truth

New Moon energy invites us to explore how we can deepen our alignment with our intentions and asks us to focus on what we want to grow and expand on in our lives. The Gate 44 brings us the ability to decipher the patterns of the past and create a deeper alignment with our personal integrity and self-worth. This can be an energy that allows us to see what has come before with fresh eyes and to use our new perspective and understanding to heal our sense of value.

With New Moon energy bringing us the courage to begin again, we are breaking free from the patterns of the past, seeing the Truth and moving forward in integrity. We are embracing our right place in the world and celebrating the unique, irreplaceable role that only we can play in the Cosmic Plan.

Challenge: To not get stuck in past patterns. To cultivate the courage to go forward without being stuck in the fear of the past. To learn how to transform pain into power and to have the courage to express your authentic self without compromise or settling.

Mastery: The ability to see patterns that have created pain. To bring awareness to help yourself and others break old patterns and transform pain into an increased sense of value and alignment with purpose.

Unbalanced: Fear and paralysis that the patterns of the past are insurmountable and doomed to repeat themselves.

Writing Assignment:

What patterns from the past are holding you back from moving forward with courage?

Do you see how your experiences from the past have helped you learn more about Who You Truly Are? What have you learned about your value and your power?

What needs to be healed, released, aligned and brought to your awareness for you to fully activate your power?

What needs to be healed, released, aligned and brought to your awareness for you to step boldly into your aligned and authentic path?

Affirmation: I am powerfully intuitive and can sense the patterns that keep others stuck in limiting beliefs and constricted action. Through my insights and awareness, I help others break free from past limiting patterns, learn to find the power in their pain, find the blessings in their challenges, and align more deeply with an authentic awareness of their True Value and Purpose.

NOVEMBER 5, 2021

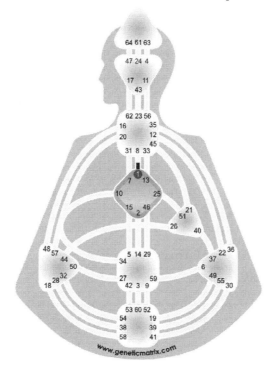

GATE 1: PURPOSE

CHALLENGE:

To discover a personal, meaningful and world-changing narrative that aligns with a sense of purpose and mission. "I am…" To learn to love yourself enough to honor the idea that your life is the canvas and you are the artist. What you create with your life IS the contribution you give the world.

JOURNAL QUESTIONS:

1. *Am I fully expressing my authentic self?*

2. *What needs to be healed, released, aligned or brought to my awareness for me to more deeply express my authentic self?*

3. *Where am I already expressing who I am?*

4. *Where have I settled or compromised? What needs to change?*

5. *Do I feel connected to my life purpose? What do I need to do to deepen that connection?*

AFFIRMATION:

My life is an integral part of the cosmos and the Divine Plan. I honor my life and know that the full expression of who I am is the purpose of my life. The more I am who I am, the more I create a frequency of energy that supports others in doing the same. I commit to exploring all of who I am.

 ## EFT SETUP:

Even though I am afraid that I am failing my life mission, I now choose to relax and allow my life to unfold before me with ease and grace. I trust that every step I take is perfectly aligned with my soul purpose and I deeply and completely love and accept myself.

NOVEMBER 11, 2021

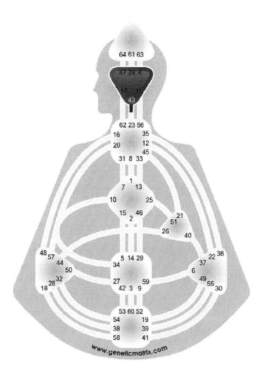

www.geneticmatrix.com

GATE 43: INSIGHT

 ## CHALLENGE:

To be comfortable and to trust epiphanies and deep inner knowing without doubting what you know. To trust that when the timing is right you will know how to share what you know and serve your role as a transformative messenger who has insights that can change the way people think and what they know.

 ## JOURNAL QUESTIONS:

1. *Do I trust in Divine Timing?*

2. *Do I trust myself and my own Inner Knowing? What can I do to deepen my connection with my Source of Knowing?*

3. *What needs to be healed, released, aligned or brought to my awareness for me to trust my own Inner Knowing?*

AFFIRMATION:

I am a vessel of knowledge and wisdom that has the ability to transform the way people think. I share my knowledge with others when they are ready and vibrationally aligned with what I have to share. When the time is right, I have the right words and the right insights to help others expand their thinking, re-calibrate their mindset and discover the elegant solutions to the challenges facing Humanity.

EFT SETUP:

Even though it's hard to wait for someone to ask me for my insights, I now choose to wait and know that my thoughts are valuable and precious. I only share them with people who value my insights and I deeply and completely love and accept myself.

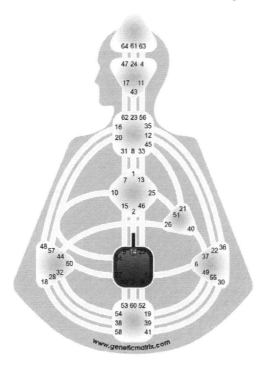

GATE 14: CREATION

 ## CHALLENGE:

To learn to trust to respond to opportunities that bring resources instead of forcing them or overworking. To learn to value resources and to appreciate how easily they can be created when you are aligned. To be gracious and grateful and not take for granted the resources you have.

JOURNAL QUESTIONS:

1. *Do I trust that I am supported?*

2. *Am I doing my "right" work? What is the work that feels aligned with my purpose? How is that work showing up in my life right now?*

3. *What resources do I have right now that I need to be grateful for?*

4. *If I didn't "need" the money, what work would I be doing?*

AFFIRMATION:

I am in the flow of Divine Support. When I trust the generous nature of the Divine and I cultivate a state of faith, I receive all the opportunities and support that I need to evolve my life and transform the world. I know that the right work shows up for me and I am fulfilled in the expression of my life force energy.

 ## EFT SETUP:

Even though I'm afraid that I can't do what I love and make money, I deeply and completely love and accept myself.

November 19, 2021 Partial Lunar Eclipse and Full Moon

 Taurus 27 degrees and 14 minutes

 Gate 8 - The Gate of Fulfillment

Full moon energy invites us to explore what we need to release and let go of in order to stay in alignment with our intentions. Eclipse energy amplifies the intensity of the Full Moon.

The Gate 8 brings us a deep need to express our Authentic Selves. The "fulfillment" of the Gate 8 is the fulfillment of the deepest expression of who we truly are. This Full Moon/ Eclipse energy gives us the power to release anything in our personal narrative that is blocking our authentic self-expression.

This is an energy that can feel pressurized, make us worry that we are "failing" our life purpose. This powerful Full Moon invites you to remember that YOU are your life purpose. It's not what you do, it's who you "BE". You being the full, authentic expression of who you are designed to be IS the contribution you are here to give the world.

There has never been anyone like you on the planet before and there will never be anyone like you again. You are a cosmic-once-in-a-lifetime-event. This Full Moon invites you to let go of anything that is keeping you from being fully authentic in your life.

Challenge: To learn to express yourself authentically. To wait for the right people to see the value of who you are, and to share yourself with them vulnerably with all your heart. To learn to trust that you are a unique expression of the Divine with a purpose and a path. To find that path and to walk it without self-judgement or holding back.

Mastery: To push the edges and boundaries of authentic self-expression and to realize that your being the full expression of your authentic self IS your life purpose. To use your authentic expression to inspire others to fulfill themselves

Unbalanced: Feeling panicked and disconnected from your Life Purpose. Thinking that your Life Purpose is something you have to "do" versus someone you have to "be". To try to be someone you're not in an attempt to serve as a "role model".

Writing Assignment:

Do you feel safe in vulnerability? What experiences have caused you to feel unsafe expressing your true self? Can you rewrite those stories?

What would an uncompromising life look like for you?

What do you need to remove from your current life to make your life more authentic?

What is one bold action you can take right now that would allow you to express who you are more authentically in the world? What is your true passion? What do you dream of?

Affirmation: I am devoted to the full expression of who I am. I defend and protect the story of my Life. I know that when I am expressing myself, without hesitation or limitation, I AM the contribution that I am here to give the world. Being myself IS my life purpose and my direction flows from my authentic alignment.

NOVEMBER 22, 2021

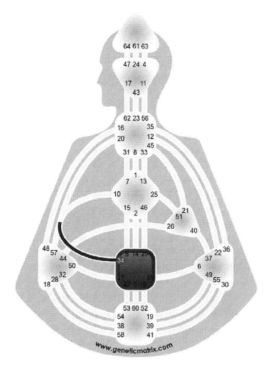

GATE 34: POWER

 ## CHALLENGE:

To learn to measure out energy in order to stay occupied and busy but to not burn yourself out trying to force the timing or the "rightness" of a project. To wait to know which project or creation to implement based on when you get something to respond to.

 ## JOURNAL QUESTIONS:

1. *Do I trust in Divine Timing? What do I need to do to deepen my trust?*

2. *How do I cultivate greater patience in my life?*

3. *What fears come up for me when I think of waiting? How can I learn to wait with greater faith and ease?*

4. *What do I do to occupy myself while I'm waiting?*

 ## AFFIRMATION:

I am a powerful servant of Divine Timing. When the timing is right, I unify the right people around the right idea and create transformation on the planet. My power is more active when I allow the Universe to set the timing. I wait. I am patient. I trust.

 ## EFT SETUP:

Even though I'm afraid to be powerful, I now choose to fully step into my power and allow the Universe to serve me while I serve it and I deeply and completely love and accept myself.

NOVEMBER 28, 2021

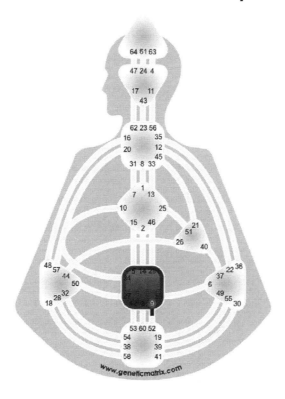

GATE 9: CONVERGENCE

 ## CHALLENGE:

The energy is about learning where to place your focus. When we work with the energy of this Gate, we have to learn to see the trees AND the forest. This Gate can make us seem "blind" to the big picture and we can lose our focus by getting stuck going down a "rabbit hole."

 ## JOURNAL QUESTIONS:

1. *Where am I putting my energy and attention? Is it creating the growth that I'm seeking?*

2. *What do I need to focus on?*

3. *Is my physical environment supporting my staying focused?*

4. *Do I have a practice that supports me sustaining my focus? What can I do to increase my focus?*

AFFIRMATION:

I place my focus and attention on the details that support my creative manifestation. I am clear. I easily see the parts of the whole and I know exactly what to focus on to support my evolution and the evolution of the world.

 ## EFT SETUP:

Even though I've been frustrated with my lack of focus, I now choose to be clear, stay focused and take the actions necessary to create my intentions.

DECEMBER 3, 2021

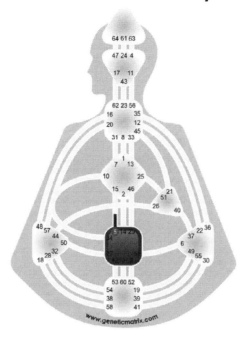

GATE 5: CONSISTENCY

 ## CHALLENGE:

To learn to craft order, habits and rhythm that support alignment, connection and the flow of Life Force energy and the fulfillment of purpose. To master staying in tune with consistent habits and alignment that support your growth and evolution no matter what is going on around you. Aligning with natural order and staying attuned to the unfolding of the flow of the natural world.

 ## JOURNAL QUESTIONS:

1. *What do I need to do to create habits that fuel my energy and keep me vital and feeling connected to myself and Source?*

2. *What habits do I have that might not be serving my highest expression? How can I change those habits?*

3. *What kind of environment do I need to cultivate to support my rhythmic nature?*

 **AFFIRMATION:**

Consistency gives me power. When I am aligned with my own natural rhythm and the rhythm of life around me, I cultivate strength, connection with Source and I am a beacon of stability and order. The order I hold is the touchstone, the returning point of love, that is sustained through cycles of change. The rhythms I maintain set the standard for compassionate action in the world.

 EFT SETUP:

Even though I feel nervous/scared/worried about waiting for Divine Timing, I now choose to create habits that support my connection with Source while I wait and I deeply and completely love and accept myself.

December 4, 2021 Total Solar Eclipse and New Moon

 Sagittarius 12 degrees and 22 minutes

 Gate 5 - The Gate of Consistency

New Moon energy invites us to explore how we can deepen our alignment with our intentions and asks us to focus on what we want to grow and expand on in our lives. Eclipse energy amplifies the intensity of the New Moon.

The Gate 5 demands order and consistency. This is the energy from which good habits are born. The energy of this New Moon invites you to explore what kinds of habits and consistent practices you need to add to your life to enhance your well-being and alignment with your Authentic Self.

The Gate 5 is the energy of natural order. This powerful New Moon/Eclipse combination invites us to not only look inward to help us establish better patterns and habits, but to also look outside of ourselves for where can create in greater alignment with nature and natural order.

We must look to the world, our Mother Earth, and explore what we need to do to live in greater harmony with nature. Is it time to change the way we eat, use our resources, decrease our waste? What visions of a clean, sustainable world do we need to hold? What new habits do we need to cultivate to better help our natural world?

Challenge: To learn to craft order, habits and rhythm that support alignment, connection and the flow of Life Force energy and the fulfillment of purpose. To master staying in tune with consistent habits and alignment that support your growth and evolution no matter what is going on around you. Aligning with natural order and staying attuned to the unfolding of the flow of the natural world.

Mastery: The ability to stay consistent with habits and choices that bring you closer to living true to who you are through alignment, and not overusing will power.

Unbalanced: Life will seem like a constant struggle to stay connected and live habitually in a way that creates stability, sustainability and a fulfilled expression.

Writing Assignment:

What do you need to do to create habits that fuel your energy and keep you vital and feeling connected to yourself and Source?

What habits do you have that might not be serving your highest expression? How can you change those habits?

What kind of environment do you need to cultivate to support your rhythmic nature?

Affirmation:

Consistency gives me power. When I am aligned with my own natural rhythm and the rhythm of life around me, I cultivate strength, connection with Source, and I am a beacon of stability and order. The order I hold is the touchstone, the returning point of love, that is sustained through cycles of change. The rhythms I maintain set the standard for compassionate action in the world.

DECEMBER 9, 2021

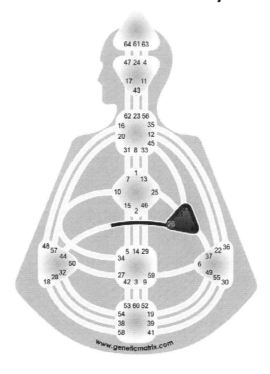

GATE 26: INTEGRITY

CHALLENGE:

To learn to value your right place and your value enough to act as if you are precious. To heal past traumas and elevate your self-worth. To trust in support enough to do the right thing and to nurture yourself so that you have more to give.

JOURNAL QUESTIONS:

1. *Where might I be experiencing a breech in my moral identity, physical, resource or energy integrity? What do I need to do to bring myself back into integrity?*

2. *When I act without integrity, can it be traumatic? What trauma do I have that I need to heal? How can I rewrite that story of my trauma as an initiation back into my true value?*

3. *What do I need to do right now to nurture myself and to replenish my value?*

AFFIRMATION:

I am a unique, valuable and irreplaceable part of the Cosmic Plan. I am always supported in fulfilling my right place. I take care of my body, my energy, my values and my resources so that I have more to share with the world. I claim and defend my value and fully live in the story of who I am with courage.

 ## EFT SETUP:

Even though I am afraid to share my Truth, I now choose to speak my truth clearly and confidently and I deeply and completely love and accept myself.

DECEMBER 14, 2021

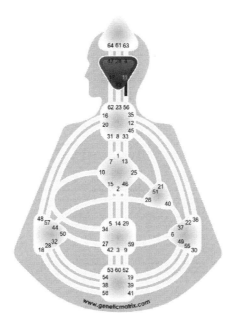

GATE 11: THE CONCEPTUALIST

CHALLENGE:

To sort through and manage all the ideas and inspiration you hold. To trust that the ideas that are yours will show up for you in an actionable way. To value yourself enough to value the ideas you have and to wait for the right people to share those ideas with.

JOURNAL QUESTIONS:

1. *What do I do with inspiration when I receive it? Do I know how to serve as a steward for my ideas? Or do I feel pressure to try to force them into form?*

2. *How much do I value myself? Am I valuing my ideas?*

3. *Do I trust the Universe? Do I trust that the ideas that are mine to take action on will manifest in my life according to my Human Design Type and Strategy?*

4. *What can I do to manage the pressure I feel to manifest my ideas? Am I trying to prove my value with my ideas?*

 **AFFIRMATION:**

I am a Divine Vessel of inspiration. Ideas flow to me constantly. I protect and nurture these ideas knowing that my purpose in life is to share ideas and inspiration with others. I use the power of these ideas to stimulate my imagination and the imagination of others. I trust the infinite abundance and alignment of the Universe and I wait for signs to know which ideas are mine to manifest.

 EFT SETUP:

Even though I've got so many ideas, I now trust that I will know exactly what action to take and when to take it and I deeply and completely love and accept myself.

December 19, 2021 - Full Moon

 Gemini 27 degrees and 29 minutes

 Gate 12 - The Gate of the Channel

Full moon energy invites us to explore what we need to release and let go of in order to stay in alignment with our intentions.

The Gate 12 has two vital functions. First of all, it is an energy that connects us deeply to the transformative power of Source. It is through this Gate that we connect to our ability to know what we need to know when we need to know it. It also gives us deep insights and the ability to transmit our knowing to others.

Secondly, the Gate 12 is a regulator for time and timing. This energy brings with it such power for transformation and change, but we can't work with the transformation it brings if the timing isn't right. We have to make the internal changes first, to find the right alignment with Source and to make the paradigm shift necessary to be able to begin the transformation that the Gate 12 brings us.

This is intensely creative energy that is regulated by mood, the emotional signal of right timing. With this energy being highlighted by the Full Moon, we are releasing our attachment to our personal timing and learning to let go and trust in Divine Timing.

When the timing is aligned, we'll be able to transform ourselves and the world around us with the power of our insights and creative expression.

Challenge: To honor the self enough to wait for the right time and "mood" to speak. To know that "shyness" is actually a signal that the timing isn't right to share your transformational insights and expressions. When the timing IS right, to have the courage to share what you feel and sense. To honor the fact that your voice and the words you offer are a direct connection to Source and you channel the potential for transformation. To own your creative power.

Mastery: To know that your voice is an expression of transformation and a vehicle for Divine Insight. The words you speak, the insights and creativity you share, have the power to change others and the world. This energy is so powerful that people have to be ready to receive it. When you are articulate, then the timing is correct. If you struggle to find the words, consider that the timing is not right, and have the courage to wait until it feels more aligned. A powerful ability to craft language and creative expressions that changes people's perceptions.

Unbalanced: The struggle to try to speak ideas into form when it's not the right time. Letting hesitancy and caution paralyze you. Trying to force ideas and words.

Writing Assignment:
How has "shyness" caused you to judge yourself?

What do you need to do to cultivate a deeper connection with Source?

What do you need to do to connect more deeply with your creative power?

Affirmation:
I am a creative being. My words, my self-expression, and my creative offerings have the power to change the way people see and understand the world. I am a vessel of Divine Transformation and I serve Source through the words that I share. I wait for the right timing and when I am aligned with timing and flow, my creativity creates beauty and Grace in the world. I am a Divine Channel and I trust that the words that I serve will open the Hearts of others.

DECEMBER 20, 2021

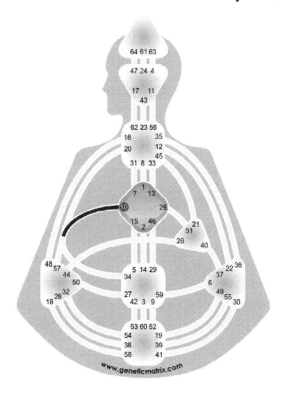

GATE 10: SELF-LOVE

 ## CHALLENGE:

To learn to love yourself. To learn to take responsibility for your own creations.

 ## JOURNAL QUESTIONS:

1. *Do I love myself?*

2. *What can I do to deepen my self-love?*

3. *Where can I find evidence of my lovability in my life right now?*

4. *What do I need to do to take responsibility for situations I hate in my life right now? What needs to change?*

5. *Where am I holding blame or victimhood in my life? How could I turn that energy around?*

 **AFFIRMATION:**

I am an individuated aspect of the Divine. I am born of Love. My nature is to Love and be Loved. I am in the full flow of giving and receiving Love. I know that the quality of Love that I have for myself, sets the direction for what I attract into my life. I am constantly increasing the quality of love I experience and sharing with the world.

 EFT SETUP:

Even though it I struggle with loving myself, I now choose to be open to discovering how to love myself anyway and I deeply and completely love and accept myself.

DECEMBER 25, 2021

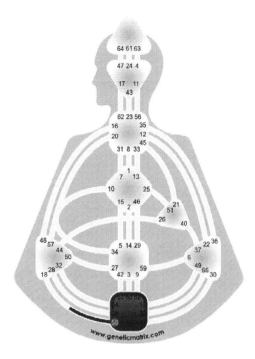

www.geneticmatrix.com

GATE 58: THE JOY OF MASTERY

 ## CHALLENGE:

To follow the drive to create the fulfillment of your potential. To learn to craft a talent and make it masterful through joyful learning and repetition. To learn to embrace joy as a vital force of creative power without guilt or denial.

 ## JOURNAL QUESTIONS:

1. *What brings me the greatest joy? How can I deepen my practice of joy?*

2. *How can I create more joy in my life?*

3. *What keeps me from fulfilling my potential and my talent? What am I afraid of?*

 **AFFIRMATION:**

I am a masterful curator of my own talent. I use my joy to drive me to master the fun expression of all that I am. I practice as my path to mastery. I know that from repetition and consistency comes a more masterful expression of my talent. I embrace learning and growing, and I commit to the full expression of my joy.

 EFT SETUP:

Even though it's hard to let go of the past, I now choose to release it and embrace all the joy that is available to me right now and I deeply and completely love and accept myself.

DECEMBER 31, 2021

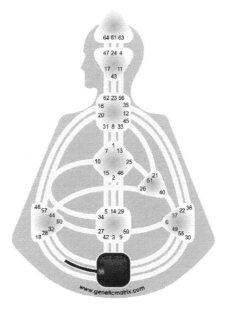

www.geneticmatrix.com

GATE 38: THE VISIONARY

 ## CHALLENGE:

To experience challenge as a way of knowing what's worth fighting for. To turn the story of struggle into a discovery of meaning and to let the power of what you discover serve as a foundation for a strong vision of transformation that brings dreams into manifested form.

 ## JOURNAL QUESTIONS:

1. *Do I know what's worth committing to and fighting for in my life?*

2. *Do I have a dream that I am sharing with the world?*

3. *Do I know how to use my struggles and challenges as the catalyst for creating deeper meaning in the world? In my life?*

 **AFFIRMATION:**

My challenges, struggles, and adventures have taught me about what is truly valuable in life. I use my understandings to hold a vision of what else is possible for the world. I am aligned with the values that reflect the preciousness of life and I sustain a vision for a world that is aligned with Heart. My steadfast commitment to my vision inspires others to join me in creating a world of equitable, sustainable peace.

 EFT SETUP:

"Even though things seem hard and challenging, I now choose to use my challenges to help me get clear about what I really want, and I deeply and completely love and accept myself."

January 2, 2022 - New Moon

 **Capricorn 12 degrees and 20 minutes**

 Gate 38 - The Gate of the Visionary

New Moon energy invites us to explore how we can deepen our alignment with our intentions and asks us to focus on what we want to grow and expand on in our lives. The Gate 38 brings us the power to hold a vision or a dream that is worth fighting for. This energy brings us the endurance and the ability to withstand the challenges ahead as we work to bring our dream into reality.

The Gate 38 invites us to explore what's really worth fighting for. With the New Moon highlighting this theme, we begin to launch ourselves - and our new calendar year - into a new endeavor to create a just and peaceful world. We are cultivating principles and values that express what's really precious in this world and we commit to taking the actions to begin to manifest these values into the world.

Challenge: To experience challenge as a way of knowing what's worth fighting for. To turn the story of struggle into a discovery of meaning and to let the power of what you discover serve as a foundation for a strong vision of transformation that brings dreams into manifested form.

Mastery: The ability to know what's worth committing to and fighting for. To use your experiences to craft a vision that anchors the possibility of something truly meaningful and worthy in the world. Serving the world as a visionary.

Unbalanced: To struggle and fight for the sake of fighting. Engaging in meaning-less fights. Aggression and struggle.

Writing Assignment:

What is something worth committing to and fighting for in your life?

What dream are you sharing with the world? What dream would you like to share?

Do you know how to use your struggles and challenges as the catalyst for creating deeper meaning in the world? In your life? In what ways could your struggles and challenges serve as a catalyst for creating deeper meaning in the world and in your life?

Affirmation: My challenges, struggles, and adventures have taught me about what is truly valuable in life. I use my understandings to hold a vision of what else is possible for the world. I am aligned with the values that reflect the preciousness of life and I sustain a vision for a world that is aligned with Heart. My steadfast commitment to my vision inspires others to join me in creating a world of equitable, sustainable peace.

JANUARY 5, 2022

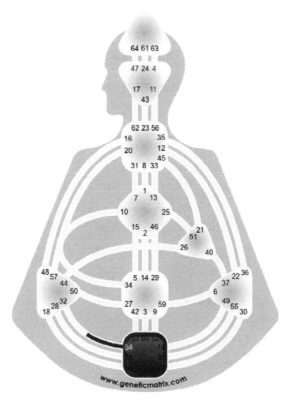

GATE 54: DIVINE INSPIRATION

 CHALLENGE:

To learn to be a conduit for Divine Inspiration. To be patient and to wait for alignment and right timing before taking action. To be at peace with stewardship for ideas and to learn to trust the divine trajectory of an inspiration.

 JOURNAL QUESTIONS:

1. *What do I do to get inspired? How do I interface with my creative muse?*

2. *Is there anything I need to do or prepare in order to be ready for the next step in the manifestation of my dream or inspiration?*

AFFIRMATION:

I am a Divine Conduit for inspiration. Through me new ideas about creating sustainability and peace on the planet are born. I tend to my inspirations, give them love and energy and prepare the way for their manifestations in the material world.

 EFT SETUP:

"Even though I'm afraid my dreams won't come true, I now choose to dream wildly and trust that my dreams will come true. All I have to do is focus my mind, trust and know that all will unfold perfectly and I deeply and completely love and accept myself."

JANUARY 11, 2022

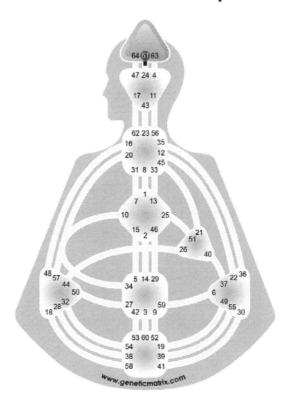

GATE 61: WONDER

CHALLENGE:

To not get lost in trying to answer or figure out why? To maintain a state of wonder. To not let the pressure of trying to "know" keep you from being present.

JOURNAL QUESTIONS:

1. *What do I do to maintain my sense of wonder? How can I deepen my awe of the magnificence of the Universe?*

2. *What old thoughts, patterns and beliefs do I need to release in order to align with my knowingness and to trust my "delusional confidence" as a powerful creative state?*

3. *What greater perspectives on the events of my life can I see? What are the greatest lessons I've learned from my pain? How do I use these lessons to expand my self-expression?*

 ## AFFIRMATION:

I have a direct connection to a cosmic perspective that gives me an expanded view of the meaning of the events in my life and the lives of others. I see the wonder and innocence of life and stay present in a constant state of awe. I am innocent and pure in my understanding of the world and my innocence is the source of my creative alignment.

 ## EFT SETUP:

Even though I don't know all the answers, I now choose to surrender and trust that I am being loved, supported and nurtured by the Infinite Loving Source that is the Universe.

JANUARY 16, 2022

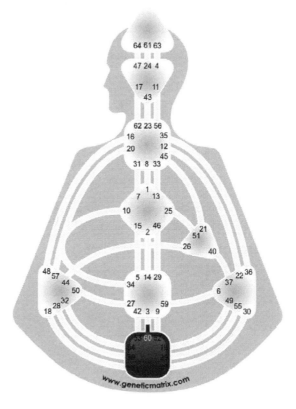

GATE 60: CONSERVATION

CHALLENGE:

To not let the fear of loss overwhelm your resourcefulness. To learn to find what is working and focus on it instead of looking at the loss and disruption.

JOURNAL QUESTIONS:

1. *What change am I resisting? What am I afraid of?*

2. *What are the things in my life that are working that I need to focus on?*

3. *Is my fear of loss holding me back?*

AFFIRMATION:

I am grateful for all the transformation and change in my life. I know that disruption is the catalyst for my growth. I am able to find the blessings of the past and incorporate them in my innovative vision for the future. I am optimistic about the future and I transform the world by growing what works.

 ## EFT SETUP:

Even though it's hard to let go of things that didn't work, I now release all the clutter from the past and I deeply and completely love, accept and trust myself.

January 17, 2022 - Full Moon

 Cancer 27 degrees and 51 minutes

 Gate 56 - The Gate of Expansion

Full moon energy invites us to explore what we need to release and let go of in order to stay in alignment with our intentions.

The Gate 56, often referred to as the "Gate of the Storyteller", reminds us that everything begins with a story, an imaginary exploration of potential and possibility. Our minds are programmed to learn from stories. We learn about the beauty of the world on the laps of the people who love us the most. This energy brings us the power to change the way we think about and see the possibilities for our life through the lens of our imagination and our engagement with new possibilities.

The Full Moon invites us to explore what we need to let go of in order to contemplate and explore new possibilities. This is not "logical" energy. It is sensual and defies old patterns from the past. We are letting go of those places where our rigid adherence to reasoning keeps us from seeing new ways of doing things. We are expanding and evolving. This Full Moon invites us to dance with possibility and potential, even if we don't know "how" to make it happen yet. For now, we're just letting our imaginations set the stage for what's next.

Challenge: To learn to share stories and inspirations with the right people at the right time. To learn to tell stories of expansion, not depletion and contraction.

Mastery: The ability to share stories and inspirations that stimulate expansive and possibility-oriented thinking in others for the sake of stimulating powerful emotional energy that creates evolution and growth.

Unbalanced: To get lost or stuck in stories and narratives that are limiting. To tell stories that contract and deplete the energy of others.

Writing Assignment:

What stories do you share repeatedly with others? Do they lift people up or cause them to contract?

What stories do you tell about yourself and your voice that cause you to either expand or contract?

What are you here to inspire others to do or be?

Affirmation:

I am a Divine Storyteller. The stories of possibility that I share have the power to inspire others to grow and expand. I use my words as a template for possibility and expansion for the world. I inspire the world with my words.

SUMMARY

Your Quantum Human Design is your key to understanding your energy, your Life Purpose, your Life Path, and your Soul's Journey in this lifetime. You are a once-in-a-lifetime cosmic event and the fulfillment of your potential and purpose is the greatest gift you can give the world.

I hope this year has been revolutionary for you and that you re-connected with the True story of Who You Are and the power and possibility of your very special life.

If you need additional support and resources to help you on your life path and soul's journey, please visit www.quantumalignmentsystem.com, where you can find Specialists and Practitioners who will help you understand the story of your Human Design chart, coach you, and help you get to the root of any pain, blocks, or limiting beliefs that may be keeping you from enjoying your Life Story. There are all kinds of free goodies, videos, e-books, and resources to help you on your way!

Thank you again for being YOU! We are who we are because you are who you are!

From my Heart to Yours,

Karen

ABOUT THE AUTHOR

Karen Curry Parker is an expert in Quantum Human Design and developed a system to help explore the relationship between Quantum Physics and Human Design. She's the creator of Quantum Conversations, a successful podcast with over 90,000 downloads in less than twelve months, and two systems of Human Design: Quantum Human Design™ and the Quantum Alignment System™. Multiple news outlets, radio shows, and tele-summits have featured her work on their programs.

Karen is also the author of numerous bestselling books all designed to help you create the life you were destined to live and find and embrace the purpose of your existence.

Karen is available for private consultations, keynote talks, and to conduct in-house seminars and workshops.

To run your chart with the new Quantum Human design language go to FreeHumanDesignChart.com & to find out more about Quantum Alignment visit https://www.quantumalignmentsystem.com/

You can reach her at Karen@quantumalignmentsystem.com.

For more great books on Human Design,
please visit our online store!

Made in the USA
Monee, IL
27 December 2020